DERBYSHIRE

SOUTHERN AREA

WALKS FOR MOTORISTS

Clifford Thompson

30 Walks with sketch maps

COUNTRYSIDE BOOKS
NEWBURY, BERKSHIRE

Countryside Books' walking guides cover most areas of England and include the following series:

County Rambles
Walks For Motorists
Exploring Long Distance Paths
Literary Walks
Pub Walks

A complete list is available from the publisher.

Originally published
by Frederick Warne Ltd

This edition published 1993

COUNTRYSIDE BOOKS
3 Catherine Road
Newbury, Berkshire

ISBN 1 85306 218 9

Sketch maps by the author
Cover photograph taken near Belper
by Andy Williams

Publisher's Note

At the time of publication all footpaths used in these walks were designated as official footpaths or rights of way, but it should be borne in mind that diversion orders may be made from time to time.
Although every care has been taken in the preparation of this Guide, neither the Author nor the Publisher can accept responsibility for those who stray from the rights of way.

Typeset by Acorn Bookwork, Salisbury, Wiltshire
Produced through MRM Associates Ltd., Reading
Printed by J.W. Arrowsmith Ltd., Bristol

Contents

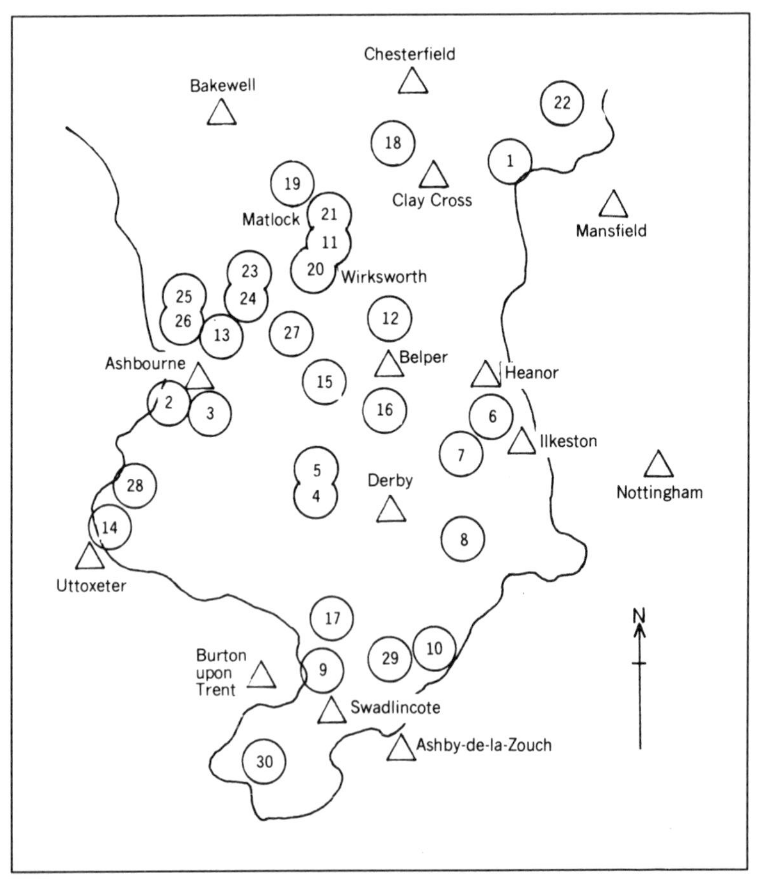

Chesterfield
Bakewell
22
18
1
19
Clay Cross
Mansfield
Matlock
21
11
20
Wirksworth
23
24
25
26
13
27
12
Belper
Ashbourne
15
Heanor
2
3
16
6
7
Ilkeston
28
5
4
Derby
Nottingham
14
8
Uttoxeter
N
17
Burton upon Trent
9
29
10
Swadlincote
Ashby-de-la-Zouch
30

Introduction

Southern Derbyshire is generally an agricultural county; there is industry and mining, but these are to be found mainly in the east, while here and there are limestone quarries. Unlike the northern part of the county there are no vast expanses of moorland, the valleys being generally shallower and less spectacular. It is an area dotted with pretty villages and there are grand houses in beautiful parklands, but the overall impression is of fields of wheat and barley, meadows bordered by tiny streams, farms nestling in hollows, hillside copses and old drystone walls.

The book has been divided into four sections highlighting various aspects of the county, but the last section obviously overlaps with the others, farming being an inescapable part of Derbyshire life. A consequence of this is the division of the land into small fields and the necessity of locating stiles or where stiles might once have been. In a lot of instances stiles no longer exist and walls or fences have to be climbed. Not all landowners are keen or even interested in preserving public footpaths and rights of way. Most of southern Derbyshire is outside the boundary and protection of the Peak District National Park and does not attract visitors as northern Derbyshire does. Few attempts are made to attract walkers and yet there are delightful walks, a selection of which are described in the book.

A sketch map is provided with each walk together with the number of the appropriate 1:50,000 Ordnance Survey map which should be used in conjunction with the walk. Better still are the 1:25,000 OS maps which are listed after the smaller scale maps. As the sketch maps are not to scale, using these with the walks makes life a lot easier, with the footpaths marked in green and greater detail of the terrain being shown.

At the beginning of each walk the grid reference of the starting place is given. These are taken from Ordnance Survey maps and for anyone not familiar with the grid system, a study of the explanatory notes on Ordnance Survey maps is useful.

How to behave when out walking is largely common sense, but it is always a good idea to remember the Country Code –

Guard against fire risk
Fasten all gates
Keep dogs under proper control
Avoid damaging fences, hedges and walls
Leave no litter
Safeguard water supplies
Protect wild life, wild plants and trees
Go carefully on country roads
Respect the life of the countryside.

Clifford Thompson
Spring 1993

PARKLAND

There are many grand houses in southern Derbyshire. Some, like Elvaston Castle and Hardwick Hall are no longer completely private residences, but many are and several have private parklands. A number of private estates, however, have public footpaths and it is possible to enjoy the woodlands and fields of these parks from the paths. The walks in this section incorporate several large estates where the public can walk. At Hardwick Park and Elvaston Castle Country Park it is possible to walk practically anywhere in the grounds. Shipley Country Park is a more recent creation and is different to the other parks in that in parts this is reclaimed land.

LOOKS LIKE GOOD WET WEATHER WALK

HARDWICK PARK

WALK 1

★

4 miles (6.5 km)

OS sheet 120, SK 46/56

In the mid to late 16th century, probably the most formidable woman in England, after Elizabeth I, was Bess of Hardwick, born at Hardwick Hall in 1518. During the course of her life she outlived four husbands, using their wealth to fulfil her ambition, amounting almost to obsession, for house building. Probably her finest endeavour was Hardwick Hall, which was built when she was in her seventies. The 'E.S.' on top of the building stands for Elizabeth Shrewsbury, for her fourth husband was the Earl of Shrewsbury. The hall and park are now owned by the National Trust and there is a charge for entrance into the hall and nearby gardens. The park, however, is open from dawn to dusk and there are car parks at the hall and at the western side of the park. It is at the latter where the walk starts and is reached from a by-road just to the west of the M1 and south of junction 29. The second turn off from the by-road is signposted 'Hardwick Park'. The starting point is the National Trust Information Centre at the entrance to the park and close to the car park (SK 453 640).

Near the car park are two lakes, Miller's Pond to the north and Great Pond to the south. It is possible to walk round both ponds, but this is not included in the described walk.

Walk along the track, passing the information centre and at a crossing gate turn left through a smaller gate, signed 'Bridlepath', and cross to another bridlepath sign partway across the field. Change direction as indicated and walk to a small gate in

WALK 1

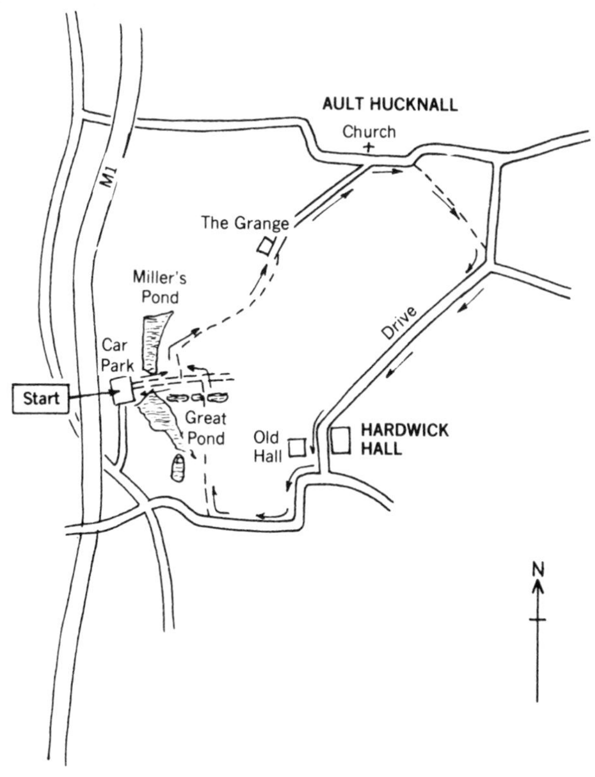

the distant fence. From here continue up the hill ahead, crossing a track to follow a path gradually bearing left to eventually join a narrow road near a house. Walk along the road to join a motor road at a church with a squat, square tower. The church has Norman origins and other historical features. The village itself is Ault Hucknall, which though small gives its name to the surrounding district.

Pass the church and at a sharp left bend enter a field on the right and cross to a stile in the middle of the opposite hedge. From here cross to the far right corner of the next field to join a road at the entrance to Hardwick Park. Walk down the long drive to the hall, passing both Bess's hall and the less imposing hall just beyond. Continue along and down the drive, round a right-hand bend, but before reaching the park exit turn right across a field, walking along a wood edge. When the fence turns left towards Great Pond, walk on in the original direction to a stile in the fence at a series of small lakes. Take the track ahead, bearing left to rejoin the track originally used and return to the information centre.

ASHBOURNE MAP 259

SNELSTON PARK

WALK 2

★

3½ miles (5.5 km)

OS sheet 128, SK 04/14

Little remains of the original Snelston Hall, but the park with its lake and woods is a delight when viewed from the public footpath passing through the eastern end of Snelston Park. The village of Snelston has its own claim to fame in that it has won a best-kept village award. Clifton, also, is an attractive village. There was once a medieval chapel but the present, rather grand, church was built in 1845. The walk starts at Clifton church (SK 165 447). Clifton lies just off the A515 south of Ashbourne.

Take the Mayfield road and just before a stream turn left on the Mayfield Yarns road. Before the narrow road crosses a stream at a right-hand bend, turn left into a field and take the path to the left of the stream flowing towards the river Dove. Before reaching the river bear left and cross the field to join the river path further downstream. Walk beside the river as far as a weir. At this point turn left away from the water through a gap in the hedge and over a stile onto a farm road. Walk along the narrow road and turn right onto a motor road. After 100 yards turn left over a stile at the sign 'Public Footpath Snelston' and climb the field aiming for the right-hand edge of a copse of evergreen trees. Follow the copse edge and over a stile and head for a small pool in the middle distance. At this point it is possible to see the village of Snelston ahead. Head for the right of a tennis court and war memorial, more recognisable as it is approached. Take the stile near the field corner close to the memorial.

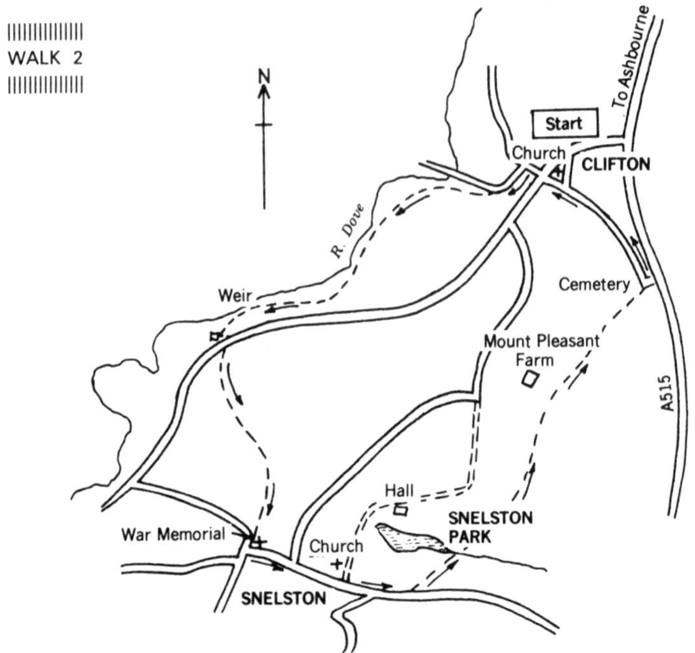

Walk along the road passing the memorial, Snelston church and the main entrance to Snelston Park. Here the top of the old hall can just be seen above distant trees. After 100 yards beyond a right turn, turn left through a stile at a sign 'Public Footpath Clifton 1' and once in the field bear right to locate a stile next to a gate in the fence between two copses. This is well to the right of the lakes. Climb the hill to the right of a copse of some 30 tall monkey-puzzle trees. Take the stile beyond to the right of the trees and cross a field to the right of a fence. Continue in this direction, passing a farm, until a road is reached just to the right of a cemetery. Turn left and walk back into Clifton.

ASHBOURNE MAP 259

OSMASTON PARK

WALK 3

★

5 miles (8 km)

OS sheet 128, SK 04/14, SK 24/34

Osmaston Manor was once a large Tudor-style mansion built in 1849 by Francis Wright, the principal owner of Butterley Iron Works. All that now remains is a curious chimney. The park that it overlooked remains and there are several attractive lakes equipped with Canada geese, greylag geese, tufted ducks and lots more. Plantations of one sort or another are evident. Near the northernmost lake is a chalet-type sawmill in an attractive setting. The nearby village of Osmaston is most attractive. The church, which lies at the opposite end of the village to the park, was built in 1845 and has obvious connections with the first owner of the mansion. In between the church and manor is the village with several thatched houses; even the village hall is thatched. The walk starts from the car park next to the village hall (SK 200 439). Osmaston is south of Ashbourne just off the A52.

Take the field path from the back of the car park, signed 'Public Footpath to Edlaston', keeping a hedge to your left and aiming for buildings on the horizon and keeping that line until a stream is crossed. Aim next for two stone gate posts halfway to the buildings and then to the right of the buildings, which are Osmaston Pastures Farm. Pass on to a road at the farm, turn left and at the T-junction ahead turn left again. After one field turn through a gate in a field and walk across the fields, with hedges to your right, aiming for the left of buildings on the horizon. Eventually climb a cart track and join a road at Wyaston.

||||||||||||||
WALK 3
||||||||||||||

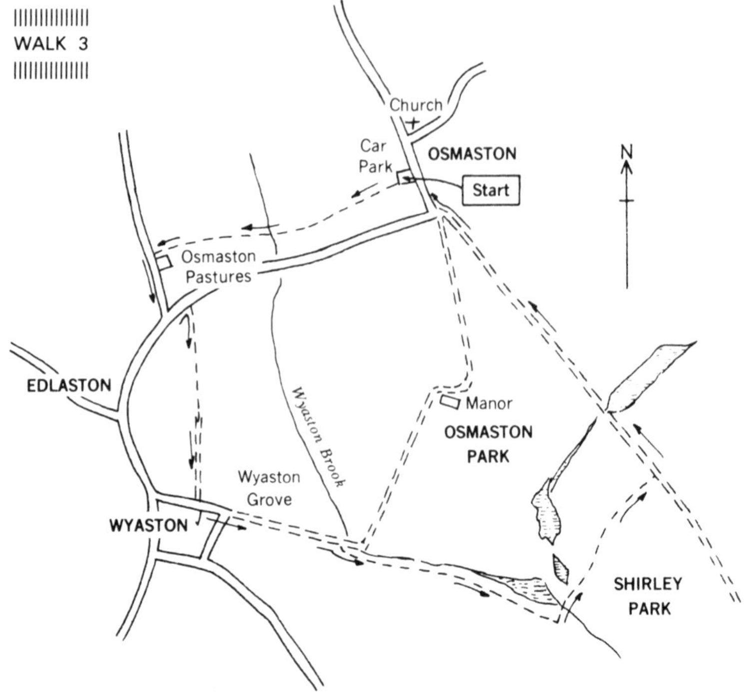

Turn left towards a white painted house. When the road turns sharp right leave it to take the track ahead and at the track end continue across the field ahead on a grass track. When a gate is reached veer right to follow the railings. A stream is soon seen at the other side of the railings and eventually a lake is seen. At the lake's eastern end take a stile next to a gate and pass on to a track to cross the stream leaving the lake. Pass the end of another lake and also the stream flowing from it. The way is now on a grass track gradually ascending and crossing other similar tracks through the plantations in Shirley Park. When a track with open fields beyond is reached turn left, descending to another of the Osmaston lakes and passing the sawmill. Cross the foot of the lake and continue on the track, at first climbing the hill; then on level ground eventually arriving at Osmaston at the village pond near the park gates. The last stretch is along the village street.

There are other ways through the park. At the park entrance is a public bridleway sign to Wyaston and the path is through the heart of the park.

WALK 4

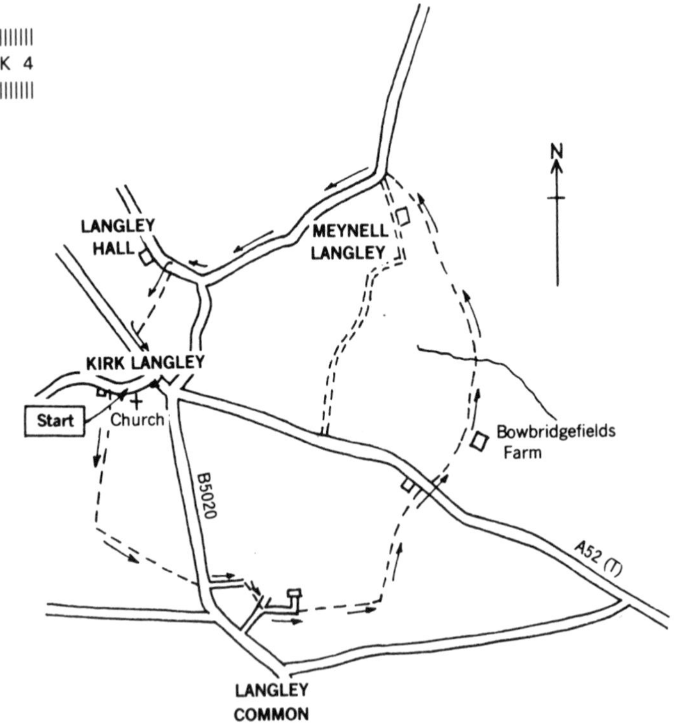

LANGLEY HALL
MEYNELL LANGLEY
N
KIRK LANGLEY
Start
Church
Bowbridgefields Farm
B5020
A52 (T)
LANGLEY COMMON

DRY WEATHER WALK JUST N.W. of DERBY OS MAP 259

MEYNELL LANGLEY PARK

WALK 4

★

4½ miles (7 km)

OS sheet 128, SK 23/33

The Meynell family, except for two brief periods, has held land near Kirk Langley since the reign of Henry I, and Meynell Langley is still the family home. The walk is around the outside of part of the park. Close to Meynell Langley is Kedleston Park with its much larger park and grander house, open to the public at bank holidays and spring and summer Sundays. The walk starts at Kirk Langley church on the road opposite the Meynell Arms Hotel (SK 287 388). Kirk Langley is a few miles north-west of Derby on the A52.

Walk further along the road and turn into the second field on the left, a narrow field next to a farm. At the end of the field enter the first field after the church and walk along the hedge side for two fields, passing through a stile at the end of the second field. Pass through a gate just ahead and walk along the right-hand side of a hedge for two fields. Climb the stile ahead, walk along the hedged grass track ahead and then along the left side of a hedge until a road is joined.

Cross the road and walk along a narrow lane signed 'Public Footpath to Mackworth'. The lane ends at a gate. Turn right over a stile next to the gate and walk along the field edge to enter a snicket at the right field corner. This follows the boundary of a house to join a narrow road at several road junctions. Cross the road and take the narrow road opposite. When the road turns left to a house, climb the fence in the road corner and the stile just beyond into a field. Bearing slightly left, aim for the left end of a low power line and climb the fence 40 yards to the right of the last pylon. Cross the next field and over a stile. Bear half left, aiming for the hedge across the field 70 yards from the left-hand corner. Locate and cross a bridge and stile. Cross to the opposite corner of the next field to join a road.

Turn right along the road for a few yards then climb a stile next to a gate into a field on the left, aiming to the left of the farm ahead. Keep to the left of the farm buildings boundary, walking to the end of the field beyond the farm and passing through a metal gate at the end of the field 50 yards to the left of the field corner. Walk to the far left corner of the next field and cross a small stream by a bridge near the field corner. Cross to the stile in the fence opposite, just to the right of a hedge. After a stile walk to the right of a hedge for several fields to join a motor road. Over the hedge is Meynell Langley Park. Over to the right is Kedleston Park. Looking back are long distance views when at least three power stations can be seen.

Turn left along the road. At a T-junction turn right and just after a left bend enter a field on the left at a gate. Walk straight across the field to a bridge over a stream. Cross two short fields ahead to join the A52. Turn left and Kirk Langley is soon reached.

N.W. OF DERBY
NOTE LENGTH 5½ MILES
BUT CUT OFF BOTTOM TO
TO TAKE
BONNIE PRINCE
CHARLIE WALK?

RADBOURNE

WALK 5

★

5½ miles (9 km)

OS sheet 128, SK 23/33

Radbourne Hall is a private house which was rebuilt in the mid 18th century and was the home of the Chandos-Pole family for three centuries before that. Although the extensive grounds are not generally accessible to the public, there is one public footpath through the park and from it the handsome red brick house can be seen, if but briefly. Happily the path passes closer to the small village of Radbourne with its school, houses, farm and 13th century church. The starting place is the medieval St Michael's church in the pleasant village of Kirk Langley (SK 287 388) a few miles north-west of Derby on the A52.

Walk to the A52, turn right and then right again along Moor Lane which is the B5020. At a road junction cross the road and walk along Poles Road, signposted 'Public Footpath to Radbourne Common 1¾'. At the end of the houses the road becomes a grassy path, soon to join a farm road at a farm. Walk along the road to a motor road. Cross the road and enter the field beyond at a public footpath sign and walk to the left of a hedge. When the hedge turns right, bear left to a stile in the hedge ahead. Beyond this cross to a stile in the fence opposite which is at the other side of an overgrown watercourse. After this cross to a stile next to an old, stunted oak tree. Cross the next field to a gate 40 yards from the opposite left corner. Bear right and cross to a stile 100 yards from the opposite left corner. Walk along the left side of the hedges of the next two fields and after another stile and a bridge in the field corner,

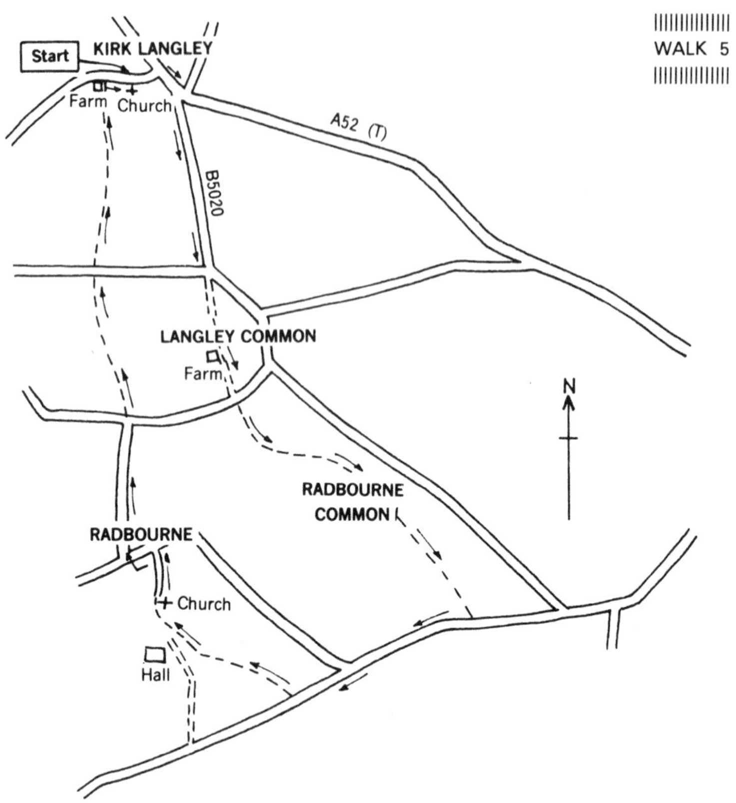

walk along the right-hand side of a hedge to join a road.

Turn right and walk along the road. The grounds of Radbourne Hall can be seen ahead and these are reached at a road junction. A quarter of a mile beyond this junction turn right at a public footpath sign and enter the grounds. After crossing a bridge a short way ahead bear left along a fence and beyond this to the right of trees and walk to the right of the hall which will soon be seen through the trees. A grass track is joined and the direction is towards the small church which is soon passed. A narrow road is joined which passes between buildings to meet a road. Turn left and after a sharp right bend take the Kirk Langley road until another road junction is joined.

Climb a stile opposite, by an old oak tree and walk up a field, which at the time of writing is a young plantation, towards a distant farm, gradually approaching a hedge on the right. In the next field bear slightly right and head for stiles and gates opposite. Walk to the left of the hedge ahead and cross the middle of the next field to a motor road. Cross the road to enter the field ahead and walk along the right-hand side of a hedge for three fields. Pass through a gate and a gap in the hedge ahead, crossing to a stile near the opposite left corner. Walk along the next hedge side to join a road. Turn right and return to the church.

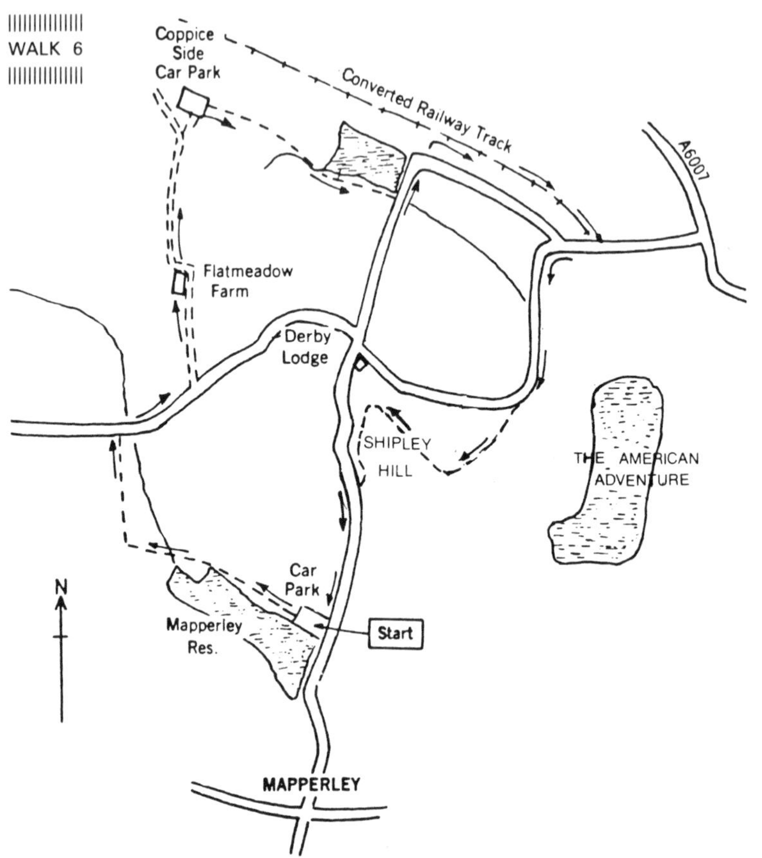
WALK 6
Coppice Side Car Park
Converted Railway Track
A6007
Flatmeadow Farm
Derby Lodge
SHIPLEY HILL
THE AMERICAN ADVENTURE
Car Park
Start
Mapperley Res.
N
MAPPERLEY

SHIPLEY COUNTRY PARK

WALK 6

★

4 miles (6.5 km)

OS sheet 129, SK 44/54

Lying between Heanor and Ilkeston, Shipley Country Park was once more noted for its mines, slag heaps and ugliness than its recreational facilities. Mines can still be seen, but the bulk of the slag heaps have largely been reclaimed. On 26th May 1976, Shipley Country Park was opened by the Derbyshire County Council. There are two lakes, Osborne's Pond and Mapperley Reservoir, and on Shipley Hill a tower which is all that is left of Shipley Hall. On the ascent of Shipley Hill there is a good view of The American Adventure theme park.

The starting point of the walk is at Mapperley Reservoir at the southern part of the park and probably best reached from the A609 through the village of Mapperley (SK 435 436).

Take the lakeside path walking west on the northern shore and at end of the reservoir, just beyond a rafted section of the path, turn right on another path to join a narrow road. Turn right on the road and take the first left turn along the farm road to Flatmeadow Farm, passing round the farm and continuing on the farm road beyond to arrive at Shipley Park Visitors Centre.

The centre is well worth a visit. There is everything here that one could wish of an information centre.

Beyond the centre bear right to pass a car park and take a hard path to the left of a fenced reclaimed mound. Beyond this rise can eventually be seen Osborne's Pond through the trees.

Walk on the right-hand side of the lake and at the road turn left towards an old railway embankment which is climbed. The track has long since been converted into a path. Turn right and walk along the path as far as houses, then leave the path to join a road on the right. Take the road heading in a southerly direction to pass 'The Inn on the Lake'.

When the road turns right to a cricket ground, walk forward past a gate to ascend a fenced road. When the road bends right, pass through a gap in the fence on the left at a wooden form to climb a path through trees. It is here that you will get the best view of The American Adventure.

When a track is reached there are various signposts. Follow the arrows to Beech Walk. At a track at the top of the hill carry on in the same direction as far as a crossroad of tracks. Turn right and head for the tower shortly seen. You are now walking over what was once Shipley Hall. Turn left at the tower to walk once again on the Beech Walk, but shortly turn right down a path to join Shipley Lane. Turn left and walk on the road back to Mapperley Reservoir.

NEAR ILKESTON
DRY WEATHER

LOCKO PARK

WALK 7

★

4½ miles (7 km)

OS sheet 129, SK 44/54, SK 43/53, SK 23/33

In medieval times Locko was a leper hospital, but since the end of the 16th century it has been the residence of various families and from 1747 the home of the descendants of John Lowe of Derby. The hall is three storeys high, of various styles and cannot be visited. The estate with its deer park has a public footpath through its length which merges with a bridleway passing the length of the lake and which provides a picturesque foreground for the hall. The walk is from Stanley, a village between Ilkeston and Derby, and reached from the A608 or A609. It starts at the Bridge Inn (SK 417 401) to the south of the village.

Walk south on the road until the road bends right, at the end of the houses beyond the Bridge Inn. Turn left up the drive to Quarry Farm, passing to the right of a farm and along the right-hand side of the hedge beyond. At the field corner turn right to a stile 50 yards before the next corner. Cross the middle of the field beyond the stile to join a farm road at the opposite left corner. Cross the track and climb the stile to the right of a gate just ahead and walk along the left side of a hedge for two fields. Climb over a fence in the second field corner and continue to the right of the next hedge to a wood. Keep to the right of the wood and soon the tower of Locko comes into view. After crossing a bridge at the extreme right of the wood, walk to the right of a fence to another denser wood. Pass through an iron gate and walk through the wood. In the field beyond walk

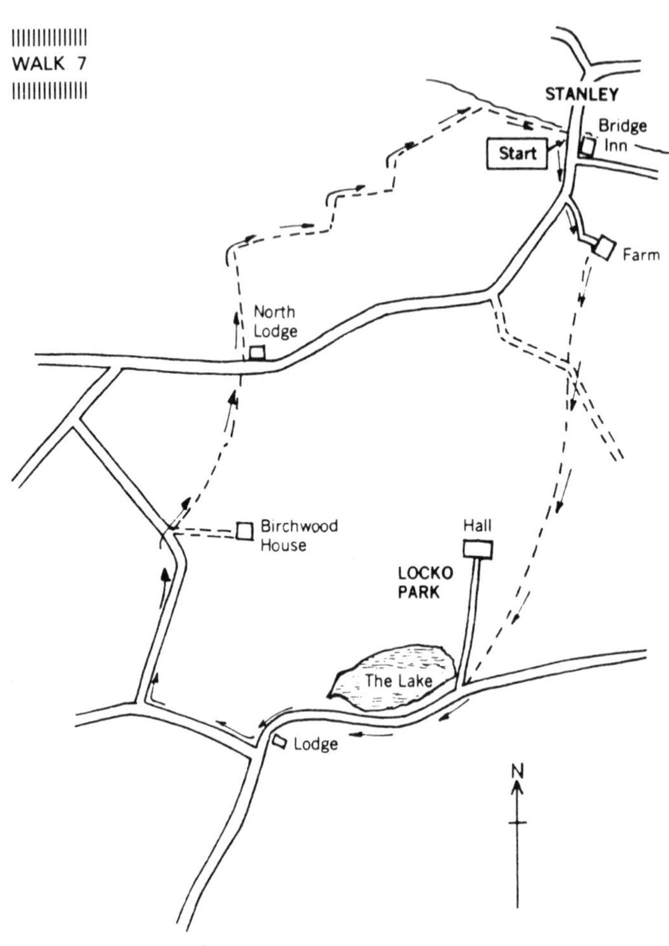
WALK 7
STANLEY
Bridge
Inn
Start
Farm
North
Lodge
Birchwood
House
Hall
LOCKO
PARK
The Lake
Lodge
N

to the road visible ahead. This is the hall drive. Turn left on the road which is alongside the length of the lake, continuing beyond the lake and passing the lodge to join a motor road.

Turn right along the road. Soon there is a right-hand bend, a long straight and then a left bend. On the straight beyond the left bend the drive to Birchwood House is reached. Turn right to cross the cattle grid and immediately left to cross a field to a stile in the field corner to the left of a wood. Walk in the field to the left of the wood and in the field corner cross two stiles to the right and continue in the same direction as before to join a road at North Lodge.

The next and last part of the walk is mainly along field edges back to Stanley. Cross the stile to the left of North Lodge and walk along the left side of a hedge, passing kennels on the way. Take the stile in the field corner and cross the next field to the far left corner, to a stile 40 yards to the right of the corner. Be wary of a ditch before the stile. After climbing the stile turn right and walk along the field edges for two fields. Turn left in the second field and walk round two sides of the field and continue on the right side of the hedge in the next field to a line of trees beyond the opposing hedge. Pass over a stile and walk to the right of the hedge for four fields. The path reaches a road at the Bridge Inn.

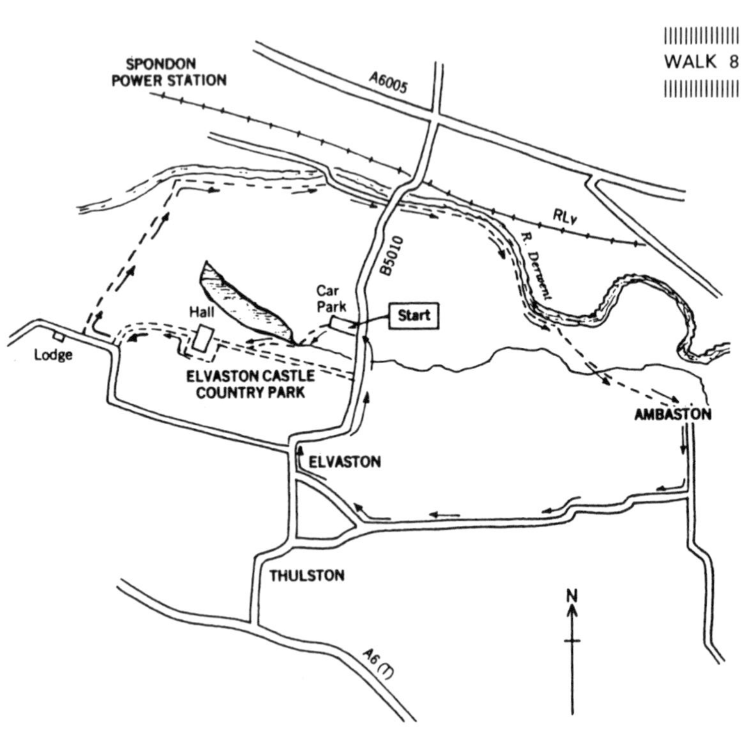
SPONDON
POWER STATION
A6005
RLy
R. Derwent
B5010
Car
Park
Start
Hall
Lodge
ELVASTON CASTLE
COUNTRY PARK
AMBASTON
ELVASTON
THULSTON
A6 (T)
N

LONGISH, MORE A DRY WEATHER WALK

ELVASTON CASTLE COUNTRY PARK

WALK 8

★

5½ miles (9 km)

OS sheet 129, SK 43/53

Elvaston Castle has a most impressive frontage viewed from the wide, grassed and tree-lined main drive and since 1970, when the grounds were designated a country park, the public has been able to enjoy the grandeur which had earlier been the sole perquisite of the Earls of Harrington. Much of the 390 acres of parkland is open to public access, for besides the grand mansion there is a picturesque lake, a high-walled old English garden, a curiously ornamented isolated building, a permanent nature trail, a caravan park, a formal garden and an estate museum. In the castle is a cafe and information bureau and there is a large scenic car park which is the starting place for the walk (SK 412 332). The park lies a few miles south-east of Derby between the A6005 and A6 roads.

Walk to the castle buildings and go round the back to a yard and take a track passing a riding school and estate museum. When just beyond the trees turn right on another track and on reaching a signpost take the track to Alvaston. Just prior to the gates leading to Castle Lodge, turn right on a recently made track to cross the countryside to the river Derwent opposite Spondon Power Station. Walk along the river bank to join the power station road. Walk on the road and turn left at the main road soon to be joined. Just before the river bridge turn into the field on the right and take the riverside path. When the river bends left after a long right bend, a pylon is reached close to the path. In the third field beyond this, leave the river to cross by field paths to Ambaston, crossing a stream on the way.

Ambaston is a small, single-road village. At the end of the village turn right to take the Thulston road. At the first road junction take the right fork. Elvaston is soon reached. Turn right and walk along the road to the car park. Or, for that matter, turn into the park to retrace your steps.

BRETBY PARK

WALK 9

★

6 miles (9.5 km)

OS sheet 128, SK 22/32

To the east of Burton upon Trent is the small village of Bretby, with its few houses, a village green and a church rebuilt in 1878. A prominent visitor to the village was Disraeli, who is commemorated in the church by a brass plaque to 'the foremost man of his age'. By far the most important building in the area is Bretby Hall, built for the 5th Earl of Chesterfield by Sir Jeffrey Wyatville in 1813–15, but which more recently has become Bretby Hall Orthopaedic Hospital. The hall grounds are extensive and are complete with a series of picturesque lakes. The walk starts in Bretby (SK 293 231).

Walk along the hospital drive and at the hospital follow the car park and footpath signs around part of the hall boundary to descend to the lakes. After crossing between two lakes climb the stile beyond and take the bridle road up the side of a wood. After this cross fields and woods, eventually to join a track near a farm. Turn right and beyond the farm follow footpath signs over stiles and along paths to join a road at a few houses. Turn left along the road and at the first left bend turn right through a stile into a field to follow a hedge on your right. At the first field corner turn right on a track, but after a few yards turn left to follow a fence on your right. When there is an open aspect in front turn left over a fence into a wooded area. Follow the hedge on the right and at the field corner turn left and walk on to the farm and road ahead.

Turn right on the road and take the first left turn. When the

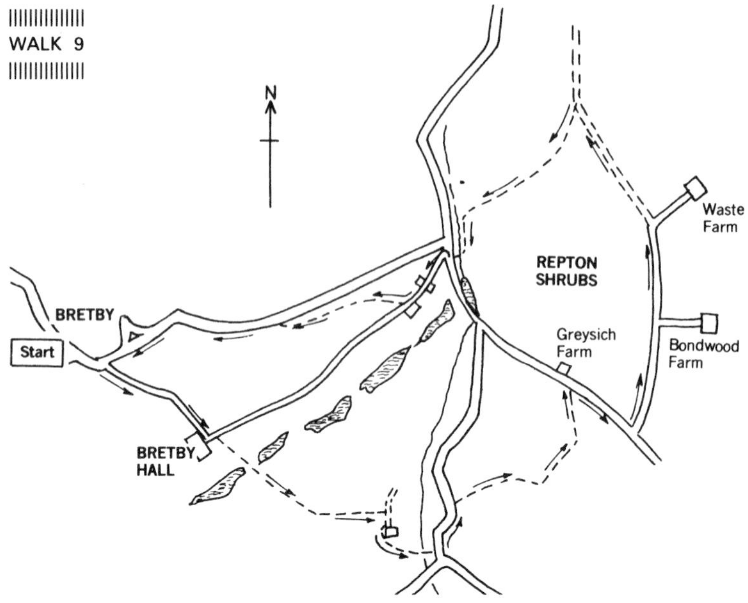

road turns sharp right to the second farm, continue instead forward on a gravelled track following the perimeter of Repton Shrubs, a large Forestry Commission plantation. At the end of the wood turn left onto a track entering the wood. Follow this and subsequent paths at the edge of the wood until a road is joined at the other side of the wood. In common with many Forestry Commission properties there is little access granted to the general public. This is the only public right of way through Repton Shrubs.

Turn right along the road and take the first left turn up another of the hall drives. Just beyond is the Bretby road. Pass through a farm and when at a house drive, pass through a gate opposite the drive into a field, crossing this and other fields, bearing left along the fields' edges, to enter a wood and descending through it to join a road. Turn left and walk back to Bretby.

BREEDON ON THE HILL

WALK 10

★

5½ miles (9 km)

OS sheets 128, 129, SK 22/32, SK 42/52

Seen from a distance the church of St Mary and Hardulph appears perched on some seaside cliff. The cliff face is actually part of extensive quarry workings. The church is older, going back to Norman times, but even the church is recent history, for it was built on the site of a Saxon monastery, and that in turn had been an Iron Age fort in the 3rd century BC. The walk is a stride into history, and also into Leicestershire for it is just over the county boundary.

The starting point is Melbourne, not quite as old as Breedon, but the history of this pleasant town would fill volumes. The more interesting part perhaps is Melbourne Hall, the home of the Marquess of Lothian – originally occupied by the Bishops of Carlisle, once leased to Charles I and later owned by Lord Melbourne, Queen Victoria's first and probably favourite Prime Minister. Melbourne in Australia derived its name in 1837 from Viscount Melbourne, who derived it from the Derbyshire town. The walk starts at the hall, near the Norman church of St Michael, which when erected was the most important church in south Derbyshire (SK 389 250).

Walk down Blackwall Lane, passing Melbourne Hall Tea Rooms. After passing over a stream and opposite a track to the left, turn right at a public footpath sign into a wooded field, crossing to a stile 40 yards from the top of the opposing hedge. Cross to the far left corner of the next field and leave the field at a cattle grid. Bear left and walk alongside a hedge on

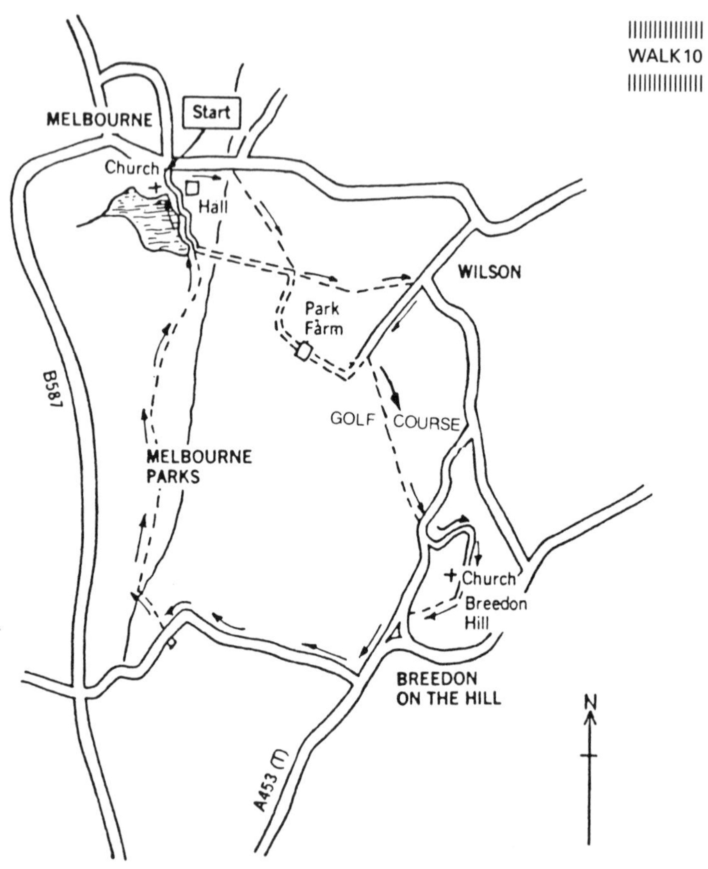

your left towards pylons at the top of the hill. It is now possible to see Breedon Hill in the distance.

Climb the fence in the field corner and, bearing left, cross the field ahead to join a narrow road to the right of houses. On the opposite side of the hedge is the golf course of Breedon Priory Golfing Centre. Turn right and walk along the road and, when power lines cross overhead, turn left onto the golf course at a footpath sign, crossing the golf course in the direction indicated by the signpost, towards the left of Breedon Hill seen clearly ahead in the distance. Beyond the golf course a road is joined near a quarry. Turn right on the road and take the first left turn up to Breedon church. The views all around are magnificent.

Locate the path at the southern end of the church and descend to the village below, walking along the main road and keeping right at the village green. Take the first right turn onto the Staunton Harold road. One hundred yards after a sharp left bend, turn right into a field at a footpath sign and a small building, walking across to the joining of a fence and hedge. Descend to the far right corner of the next field, cross the stream and stile beyond, turning right to follow the direction of the stream.

Although the outward objective was Breedon Hill, the return is through an area of parkland known as Melbourne Parks, commencing with the walk along the old Park Drive and continuing along the pleasant valley to complete the circle of Melbourne Hall and its grounds.

Walk along the valley, at first at a wood edge and later a hedge, crossing near a farm to walk to the left of another wood until Melbourne Pool is reached and beyond that the hall.

WATERWAYS

The river Trent is Derbyshire's major river, flowing generally from west to east and on its way swallowing up other Derbyshire rivers. The first to be absorbed is the Mease, which for part of its journey provides the boundary between Derbyshire and Leicestershire and Staffordshire. The second is the Dove, which for most of its way south is the boundary between Derbyshire and Staffordshire. A more central river emptying itself into the Trent is the Derwent, which starts life in the hills of the north. The last is the Erewash, the boundary line between Derbyshire and Nottinghamshire.

There are several canal systems in the county, which once briefly provided a major communication system throughout southern Derbyshire. They are now hardly required for their original purpose of carrying freight. Instead they are used for leisure. The Trent and Mersey Canal carries a regular traffic of pleasure craft and the Cromford Canal is being reclaimed.

Several of the waterways are incorporated in the following seven walks, providing delightful additional scenery to the rural landscape. It is not always possible to walk close to the water, particularly the larger rivers, but even a distant view can be an attraction.

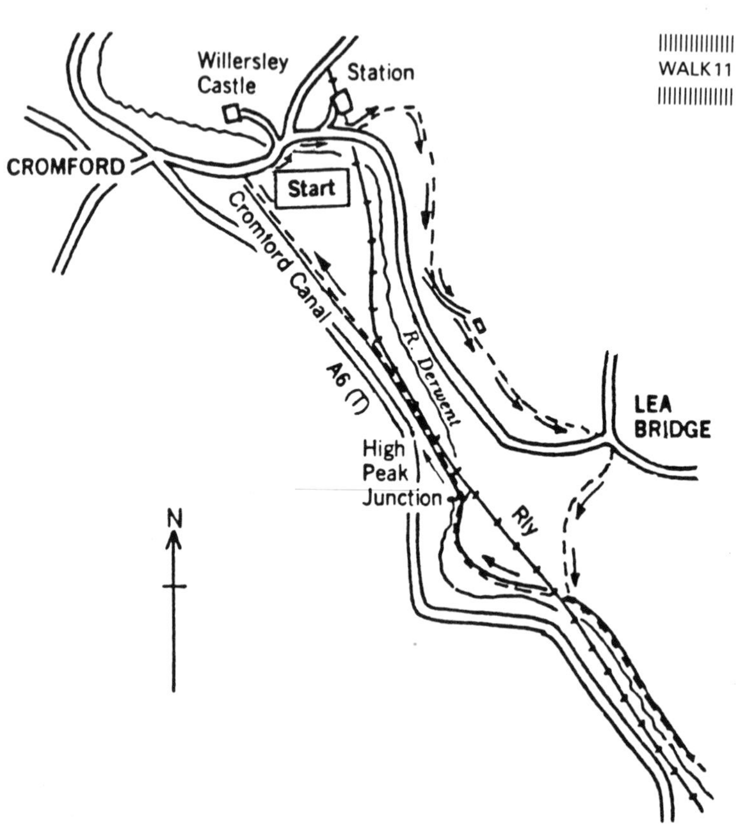
WALK 11
Willersley Castle
Station
CROMFORD
Start
Cromford Canal
R. Derwent
A6 (T)
LEA BRIDGE
High Peak Junction
Rly
N

LOOKS GOOD
NOT TOO FAR AWAY

YELLOW
MAP
24

CROMFORD CANAL

WALK 11

★

4 miles (6.5 km)

OS sheet 119, White Peak

In 1772 Richard Arkwright established the first successful water-powered spinning mill and built the village of Cromford to house his work people. In 1793 the canal opened at a cost of £80,000, a 14½ mile stretch connecting Cromford to the Erewash Canal. The railway followed later. As with most canals the Cromford Canal fell into disuse, but the Cromford Canal Society has put in a lot of good work restoring the waterway and together with the renovated buildings and all the other restored historical buildings round about, the area is an industrial historian's paradise. The walk starts from the car park at Cromford Wharf (SK 300 570).

Turn right along the road, crossing over the river Derwent and passing the drive to Willersley Castle, once the home of Richard Arkwright, but now a Methodist Guild guest house. After passing under the railway bridge turn left into a field at a signpost 'Public Footpath to Lea and Dethick'. Climb the path ahead for 200 yards and take a stile into a wood on the right. The path is through the wood and emerges into a field. Skirt the wall on the right and descend the field beyond. In the distance a lane can be seen disappearing into trees. Aim for this point and take the stile on to the lane. Turn left to climb the lane and turn right on a path that goes on the underside of a house boundary to enter a wood. The pronounced path goes through the wood and eventually descends to a motor road at Lea Bridge near a garage and not far from John Smedley's mill shop.

Just past Smedley's car park, which is opposite the road leading to the mill shop, turn right on a track and right again on a joining track to walk eventually beside a ditch that could well have been at one time a canal extension. This leads to the Cromford Canal, which is joined at the aqueduct that crosses the river Derwent. Turn right and walk along the canal towpath all the way back to the car park at Cromford Wharf.

SHINING CLIFF WOODS

WALK 12

★

6 miles (9.5 km)

OS sheet 119, White Peak

Between Whatstandwell and Ambergate, north of Belper, the past and present avenues of communications run as close together as it is possible: the trunk road, the railway and the Cromford Canal. Within a stone's throw is the river Derwent. High to the east is the village of Crich with its celebrated Tramway Museum. To the immediate west is a large expanse of National Trust woodland called Shining Cliff Woods. The route is through the wood, above it, and returns along the canal towpath. The walk starts at Ambergate station (SK 349 517), which is near to the junction of the A610 with the A6.

Descend to the A6, turn left and take the first right turn at Ambergate church. After crossing the river bridge take the first right turn on an unfinished road through woodland. When the track splits take the right fork, soon walking between the buildings of a wire works. When well beyond the works into Shining Cliff Woods proper, turn left on to a path at a fire broom stand and make the gradual ascent up the wood. At the wood end climb the stile and, bearing right, continue on the ascending path over the fields, arriving at a war memorial. At the road beyond turn right and opposite the entrance to a school and church turn left along a track. The school, a three-storeyed Georgian building, used to be the home of the Hurts, a well known county family who became pioneer ironmasters and industrialists in the 18th century.

When the track forks take the right branch. Eventually the

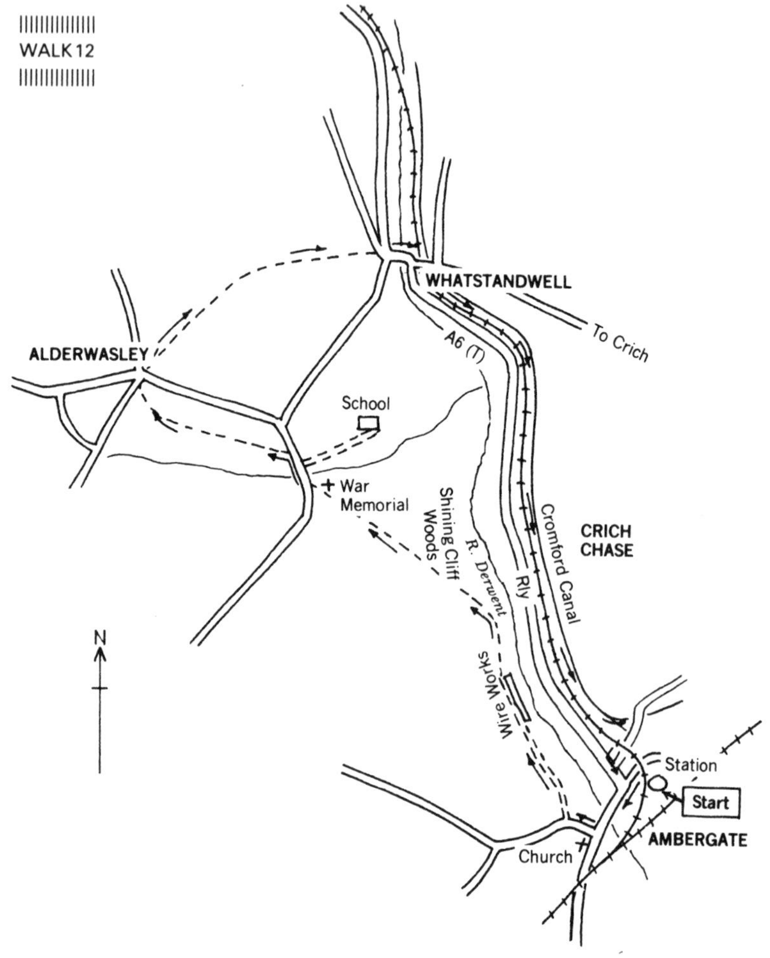
WALK 12
WHATSTANDWELL
To Crich
ALDERWASLEY
A6 (T)
School
War Memorial
Shining Cliff Woods
R. Derwent
Rly
Cromford Canal
CRICH CHASE
N
Wire Works
Station
Start
AMBERGATE
Church

path reaches a road junction at Alderwasley. Take the track to the right of Alderwasley Lodge and almost immediately right over a stile at the sign 'Public Footpath to Whatstandwell'. Cross the field to a stile to the right of a hedge fence and walk across the next field to a stile 30 yards to the left of the right-hand corner. Cross the next field to the opposite side and take the path to the right of the wood immediately ahead. A wall on the left is reached and followed to a stile which is climbed and the walk continued on the other side of the wall. Always ahead on the skyline is Crich Stand, the war memorial of the Sherwood Foresters. When a wall crosses the descent, pass through a gate to the right of a wood and continue the descent to join a track beyond a house. Walk down the track to join a narrow road and then the A6 below. Cross the river and take the Crich road for a short while, turning right to walk on the towpath of the Cromford Canal.

When the canal leaves the railway and road, and after what was once a canal basin, leave the canal at the next bridge and turn right down the narrow road to the A6. Turn left along the main road, soon reaching the turn off to the station.

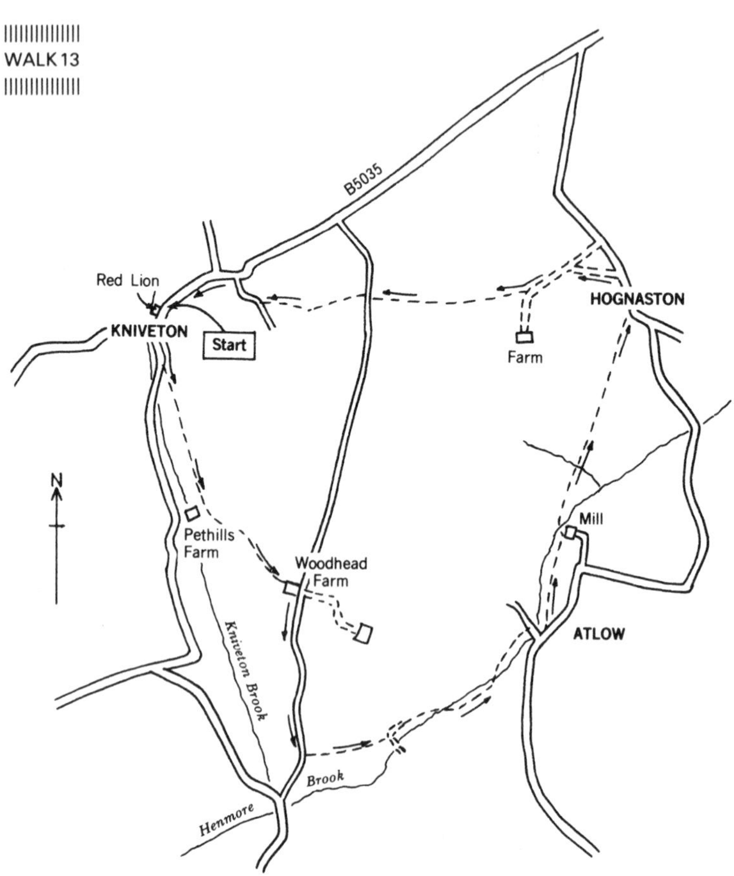
WALK 13
B5035
Red Lion
KNIVETON
Start
HOGNASTON
Farm
N
Pethills
Farm
Woodhead
Farm
Kniveton Brook
Mill
ATLOW
Brook
Henmore

Too FAR OUT

HENMORE BROOK

WALK 13

★

6 miles (9.5 km)

OS sheet 119, White Peak, SK 24/34

The valley through which Henmore Brook flows is pleasantly wooded and in parts thickly wooded. The brook eventually passes through Ashbourne to swell the waters of the river Dove at Church Mayfield. The walk starts at Kniveton, a village on the B5035 Ashbourne-Wirksworth road. Kniveton is attractive with grey stone houses and a church with a variety of historical features. The starting point is the Red Lion inn (SK 207 502).

Take the Offcote road near the Red Lion and after passing out of the village turn left up a track just past a house call Bank Side. At a left bend leave the track and pass into a field through a stile to cross the field in the same direction, passing through narrow iron gates. After an open field, and on crossing a tiny stream, walk to the left of a hedge and then above two buildings. Cross an open field, heading for the bottom right corner. Skirt the farm approached gradually, climbing the hill and passing through a stile 30 yards from the field bottom. Climb on in the same direction to a gate well up the distant hedge. After the gate, cross a field to climb a stile at a small stream and walk along the underside of the next hedge. Climb over the fence in the field corner and walk directly towards and through the farm ahead and along the farm road to join a similar road.

Turn right and walk almost to the bottom of the hill. About 100 yards before a road junction turn left over a fence stile at a public footpath sign in a hedge gap to cross a field, very gradually approaching the stream below. Beyond the ruin at this point, leave the track through a gate and cross a field, keeping to its top side. Descend the second field to cross the stream by a bridge. Follow the stream and recross it at the next bridge near an old barn. Continue upstream, passing an over-grassed moat and walk up to Atlow, another pleasant Derbyshire hamlet.

Turn right over the stream and turn left along the Hognaston road. After passing a three-storeyed house turn left through a gate and walk upstream again as far as Atlow Mill.

Cross the stream, bearing right up a track to cross a smaller stream over a bridge. Continue across the next field to a stile halfway up the opposite hedge. The village of Hognaston now comes into view. Cross fields and stiles to cross a narrow stream at a gate. Turn into a field and walk along the first hedge side, then climb directly to the houses to enter Hognaston. This is a similar village to Kniveton, having a church with a Norman font and door and 13th century tower.

Walk through the village and prior to the speed derestriction sign turn left up a track. When this joins another track turn left along it and when a farm comes into view beyond a gateway and the track descends to the farm, bear slightly right up the hill to a stile 50 yards to the right of the left corner of the field. Cross the field beyond the stile and go through a gap in the next hedge to the left of a gate. Cross to the far left corner of the field. Repeat this in the next field to join a track. Walk along the track and at its junction with another track turn left into a field and walk to the far left corner where a fence will have to be climbed. Walk along the hedge side to its right to join a farm road. This goes to Kniveton. Turn left and walk down the hill to the Red Lion.

TOO FAR OUT

THE STAFFORDSHIRE WAY

WALK 14

★

6 miles (9.5 km)

OS sheet 128, SK 03/13

The Staffordshire Way is a 90 mile, long distance walk that spans the length of the county between Mow Cop and Kinver Edge. Staffordshire County Council have created the walk and have produced books describing it and other suggested shorter walks along the Way. Part of the Way is in Derbyshire between Dove Bridge east of Uttoxeter and Abbotsholme School. The walk starts at Dove Bridge. There is a lay-by 200 yards west of the bridge on the A50 (SK 104 345).

Cross the river by the old bridge and descend to a stile into a field. Bear half right and walk towards the right of a wood and field corner. The path passes close to the river. After climbing the stile in the field corner, follow the hedge to the right and when a copse is reached climb the fence into the next field and continue in the same direction as before with the hedge to the left, eventually entering a narrow road. Cross the road and enter the next field by the gate and continue in the same direction up the field, aiming 50 yards to the right of a low corrugated barn. Climb the field beyond to the right of a hedge and emerge onto the top of the hill. Ahead is a white painted ordnance column which is to be passed. Upper Eaton Farm lies ahead.

In the field before the farm bear right and head for a gate halfway along the next hedge. Pass through the gate, bear left and aim for the right of a hedge across the field and then to the right of a wood on the skyline. At the wood is a small pond. Pass

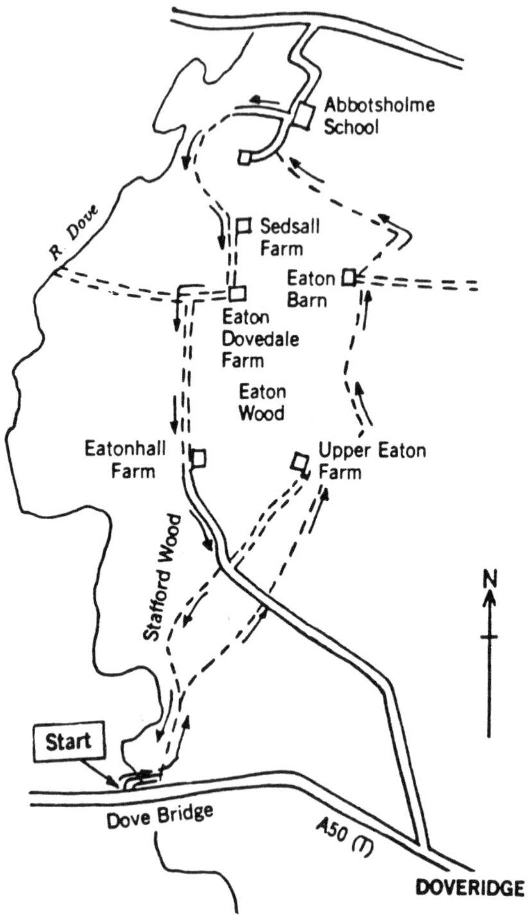

through a gate at the other side of the pond and walk around the wood edge. After another pond and a hollow in the wood edge pass through a gate. The way can now be seen ahead. Walk along the hedge, heading directly for Eaton Barn Farm. Walk up the right-hand side of the hedge. At the farm walk part way along the farm road and then bear left across the field to the far corner. In the next field cross diagonally, aiming for a white house in the middle distance. After passing through a gap in the hedge in the field corner turn sharp left and head for the left of a hedge on the skyline, with a pole apparently sticking out of its top. At this point Abbotsholme School can be seen over to the right. Walk down the left side of hedges down the fields until a farm is reached. Turn right and walk along the farm road to Abbotsholme School.

Take the first left turn after the tennis courts and descend to the fields at the end of the road. These are the school's sports fields with pitches and tennis courts. Turn left and walk across the field, gradually approaching the river. After crossing a bridge over a narrow stream cross the next large field keeping to a wood edge, eventually joining a farm track and shortly afterwards passing through Sedsall Farm. Continue on the farm road to Eaton Dovedale Farm and at the end of the farm drive turn left to follow the sign 'Public Bridle Road to Doveridge'. The grassed track passes through Eatonhall Farm and climbs a hill through trees. After passing through a gate at the top of the hill turn right into a field as indicated by the signpost 'Staffs Way' and follow the edge of the wood, eventually descending to the river to rejoin the original path.

TURNDITCH AND WINDLEY

WALK 15

★

4½ miles (7 km)

OS sheet 128, SK 24/34

Turnditch and Windley are two attractive villages to the west of Belper and the walk around the district includes a walk by the river Ecclesbourne, a narrow, winding river of no great length but of quiet, rural charm. Turnditch is the larger of the two villages and has a single road running through. An interesting building opposite the church is the quaint little school with a small bellcote. The walk starts at the church (SK 295 466).

Take the passageway next to the church opposite the school, walking to the back of the church and its graveyard into a field. Follow the path down the field as far as a bridge visible from the top of the hill. Cross the river, turn right and walk downstream following the river's course, arriving at a road bridge. This is the road from Turnditch. Cross the road and continue on the river path with the gradually approaching railway on the left. When the railway and river meet climb a stile and cross the railway, observing the WARNING sign, and walk across the field ahead to the farm and join a road.

Opposite Postern Lodge Farm drive, pass through a gated track and recross the river and railway, crossing the first field to the first hedge on the left. Climb the hill to the right of the hedge, joining a road to the right of houses. Turn left and walk through Windley until the road crosses a stream at a sharp bend in the road. Towards the bottom of the hill on the right is a large garden and in it are a number of heraldic sculptures.

Just before the road crosses a stream, turn right on the track

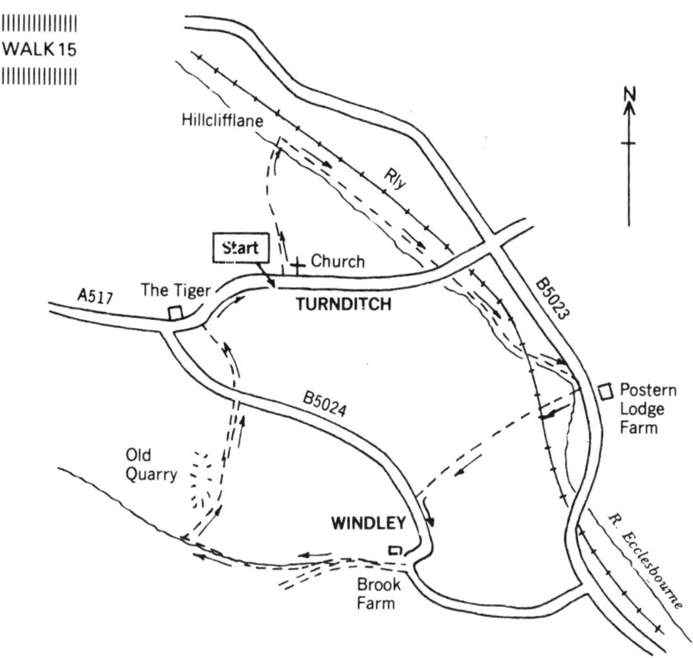

signed Corkley Cottage and walk almost as far as a stream. Prior to the stream turn right to follow a line of posts across a field, which lead to a bridge over the stream. Cross the bridge and turn right to follow the course of the stream. After a while recross the stream by a fallen tree and continue upstream until overgrown quarry workings are reached. Turn right and walk up the track to join the B5024.

Cross the road and enter fields through a stile, following stiles and yellow markers, to join the A517 to the right of the Tiger Inn. Turn right and descend into Turnditch.

WALK 16

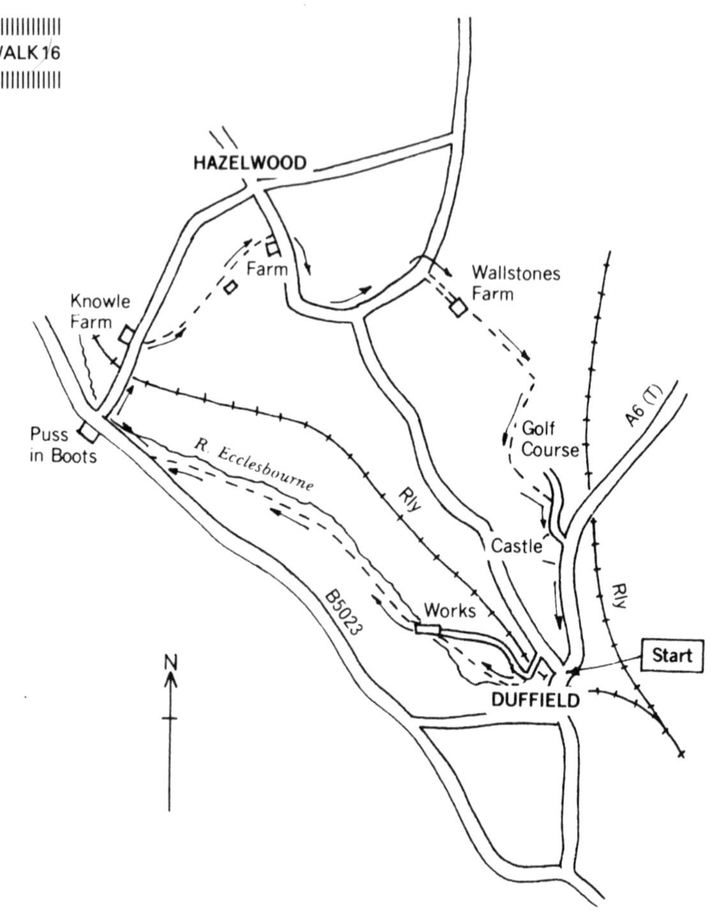
HAZELWOOD
Farm
Wallstones
Farm
Knowle
Farm
Puss
in Boots
R. Ecclesbourne
Rly
Golf
Course
A6 (T)
Castle
Rly
B5023
Works
Start
N
DUFFIELD

FAIR LENGTH
SOME GRADIENT

PUB ON WAY!
MAP 259
EAST SHEET

THE ECCLESBOURNE VALLEY

WALK 16

★

5½ miles (9 km)

OS sheet 128, SK 24/34

The river Ecclesbourne rises south of Wirksworth and makes its short journey to join the river Derwent at Duffield. It is never very wide or wild and is in keeping with its rural setting of fields and trees. The walk starts at Duffield (SK 345 435), a town on the A6, the Derwent and the railway and having ancient connections, mainly with the Normans, but going further back to Saxon times.

From the Midland Bank on the main road walk up King Street, indicated as the road to Hazelwood, and just past the Methodist chapel turn left past the Pattern Makers Arms and then right at the next junction. Shortly after, turn left on the riverside path, eventually joining another road. Continue on the road and the river bridge, passing through a stile, and walk on the path on the same side of the river as before, arriving eventually at a factory. Turn left at the sign 'Public Footpath Wirksworth Rd ½'. Pass corrugated buildings and a small detached house into a field. Walk across the field to a footpath sign and continue past it, bearing slightly right to a stile near the river. Join a track and, just before a field, turn left over a stile and walk alongside a hedge to your right, rejoining the river. Continue near the river on a path, joining the B5023 opposite a red brick bungalow 100 yards before the Puss in Boots Inn. Turn right on the road and right at the pub on to the Hazelwood road.

Opposite the entrance to Knowle Farm turn right over a stile into a field at the sign 'Public Footpath to Hazelwood ¾'. Cross the field to the stile in the opposite corner. Turn left and walk to a stile in the distant hedge and continue climbing the hill in this direction, bearing right near a house on the right to join a road after passing through a farm. Turn right and take the first left road to turn on the Belper road. When the Spring Hollow road sign appears on the road side, turn right on a track that after a short while goes round the back of Wallstones Farm. The track soon becomes a path. Walk on the path and, when this is joined from the left by another path, turn right through a stile to descend the field and walk round the boundary of Chevin Golf Club until a narrow road is reached. Walk on the road, passing the clubhouse, eventually joining the A6. Walk back into Duffield.

At the junction of the golf club road and the A6 is Castle Hill, owned by the National Trust, a high mound and the remains of Duffield Castle, once a Norman castle and occupied before then.

REPTON

WALK 17

4 miles (6.5 km)

OS sheet 128, SK 22/32

The impression about Repton is that it exists because of Repton School. Certainly the school has been there since 1557 and was built on the ruins of the priory gutted at the time of the dissolution of the monasteries. Repton, however, is ancient and is reputed to have been the capital of Mercia. The Danes followed and later in 1172 an Augustinian priory was founded. The crypt of the parish church is of Saxon origin and is one of the best surviving examples of its type. The walk starts at the parish church of St Wystan (SK 302 271).

Walk along the road out of Repton and, after passing another church at a right-hand bend, turn left onto a path to playing fields. When a narrow road is joined turn right, but after a few yards prior to the first house climb steps to the left to enter a field. Bear right and walk across the field with playing fields to the left. Pass through the gap in the field corner and walk along the side of a hedge, this time with the hedge on your right and shortly after with the hedge on your left. Now the walk for much of the way ahead is elevated above the river Trent, a continuously winding river.

At the fence end cross a short patch of open field to the top of a wood, eventually to climb a stile and walk along the other side of a fence at the edge of the wood. When the hedge ends, pass through a gate and walk around the edge of the next field towards the village now seen in the distance. Cross a narrow water channel by a plank bridge and over the stile ahead, then

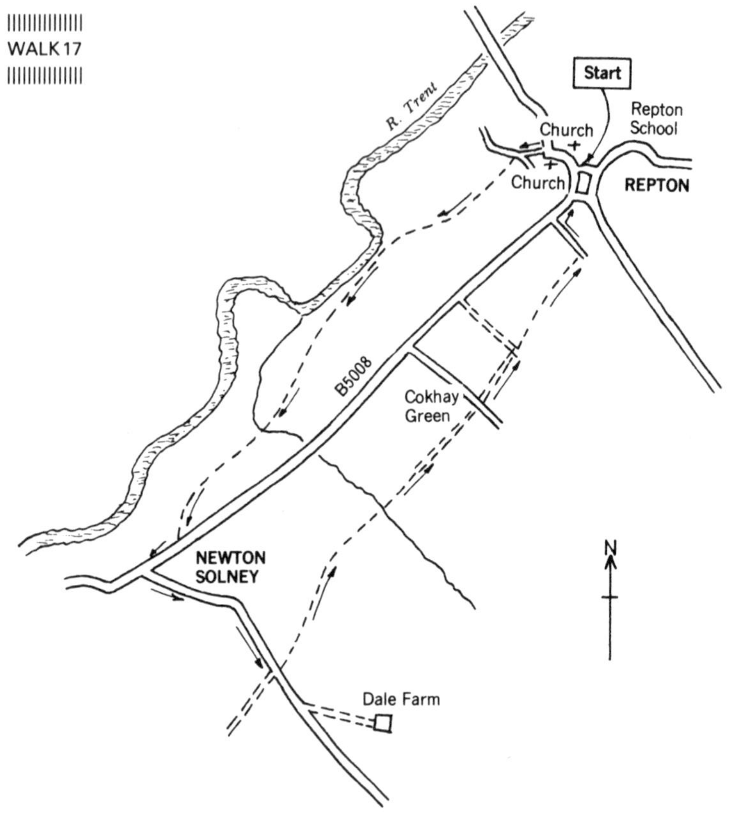

cross the next field and over another stile. Bear slightly right and cross to the middle of the hedge ahead. Climb the stile, then bearing right again cross to a fence stile halfway along the hedge to your right. Beyond this head for the far corner of the field and climb the fence stile to join a road at the village of Newton Solney. Newton Solney has its own history. Its church has Norman origins and nearby is the large, early Victorian Newton Park. The mansion is now a hotel.

Turn right along the road and left at the crossroads ahead. Well before a farm on the left climb over a stile into a field at a public footpath sign and walk across the fields with a hedge to your left. The walk is back to Repton in an unvarying direction, at first with the hedge on the left. At a copse an open field is crossed to a stile to join a hedged track. When the track meets another track enter the field ahead and walk to the right of hedges. Prior to houses, cross an open field and pass between houses to a road. Turn left and at the T-junction ahead, turn right and walk back to Repton.

VIEWPOINTS

There is little high land in southern Derbyshire. Few places are higher than 1,000 ft above sea level and these are to the north. In fact, south of Ashbourne very little land reaches even 1,000 ft and the further south the lower lies the land. Not that the countryside is flat; rather it is undulating. It comes as a surprise, therefore, when it is possible to see a long way.

The four walks in this section contain viewpoints, either distant views or, as in the case of Black Rock, bird's-eye views.

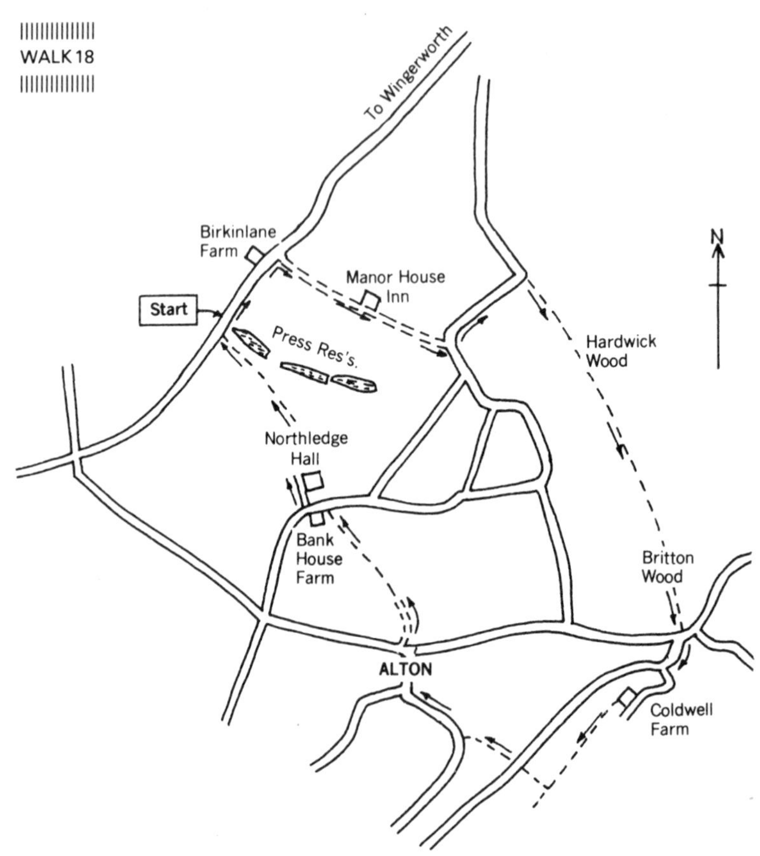
WALK 18
To Wingerworth
Birkinlane Farm
Manor House Inn
Start
Press Res's.
Hardwick Wood
N
Northledge Hall
Bank House Farm
Britton Wood
ALTON
Coldwell Farm

HARDWICK WOOD

Walk 18

★

4 miles (6.5 km)

OS sheet 119, SK 26/36

Between Wingerworth and Ashover lies an attractive area of agricultural land and woodland which is surprisingly elevated. From several places on the walk are distant views to the north and east. The starting point is at the foot of the most westerly of the three small Press Reservoirs, on the road from the A632 Matlock-Chesterfield road and Wingerworth (SK 354 657).

Take the road towards Wingerworth, climbing the hill to Birkinlane Farm. Here is a fine viewpoint to the north over and beyond Chesterfield. Fifty yards beyond the farm turn right on a track. Soon views to the east over Clay Cross can be seen. An old, isolated inn dated 1669, the Manor House Inn, is passed on the way to a motor road. Turn left to climb the road to Hardwick Wood and at a sharp left bend at the wood turn right into the wood at a public footpath sign. Take the prominent path through the wood and at its end pass through a stile into a field, walking with a wall to your right for several fields to enter Britton Wood. The path deviates slightly, but generally continues in the same direction to join a road near a junction.

Go forward to a road junction and turn right onto the Littlemoor and Ashover road. Take the first left turn signposted to Coldwell Farm, passing over a stream and climbing the hill beyond to Coldwell Farm. Pass through the middle of the farm and up the field beyond to the wood boundary wall and fence to walk by the wall. Pass through a stile and across the next field. Halfway across the next field turn right through a stile to descend through the wood and field beyond to join a road. Cross the road and over a stile to climb to the top of a field to join a narrow road. Turn right and walk to the small farming village of Alton.

Pass the first left turn to Littlemoor. Turn left on the Stone Edge road at the telephone kiosk. Take the first right turn passing between farm buildings, where the road becomes a track, passing an overgrown quarry and continuing across fields. When the track ends in a field continue in the same direction and in the field before a farm pass through a stile in a wall on the left, passing the farm to join a road.

Turn left and at the first fork turn right at a public footpath sign opposite Bank House Farm. Pass round the left side of the farm ahead, going round the corner of the farm buildings and along the left side of the wall in the first field beyond farm buildings. Cross fields to the west of Press Reservoirs now seen ahead, walking eventually on the outside of the reservoir boundary wall. The path soon reaches the road at the start of the walk.

Too far away
N. of Matlock

LUNTER ROCKS

WALK 19

★

7½ miles (12 km)

OS sheet 119, White Peak

Set amidst a few trees, Lunter Rocks are an outcrop of rocks pushing out from the ground above the village of Winster. The rocks are hardly remarkable, but the views to the north are. The walk starts at Darley Bridge picnic area next to the cricket ground on the B5057 approach road from the A6 to Darley Bridge (SK 270 623).

Walk into and through the village, turning right over the bridge. Turn right on the Stanton Lees road opposite the post office, left at the first fork and left at the second fork on this road. The roads narrow progressively and at the last turning point the road surface ceases to be a smooth, metalled surface. There is also a small triangular plot of land at the road fork. Descend with power lines towards a stream, keeping to the top side of an old tip. Before reaching the stream bear right, keeping to the right-hand side of the stream. The path now wanders near the stream through Clough Wood, eventually crossing the stream and leaving the wood at a stile near the bridge over another stream. Climb the hill ahead to the top corner and cross the stile near the corner continuing up the hill, veering slightly left until a road is reached. Turn right and walk into Winster.

Winster is an old mining village with several interesting buildings, notably the Market House owned by the National Trust. This small, two-storeyed building has an upper floor of brick and belongs to the 17th century, but the ground floor is medieval stone with painted, once open, arches. The building is

WALK 19

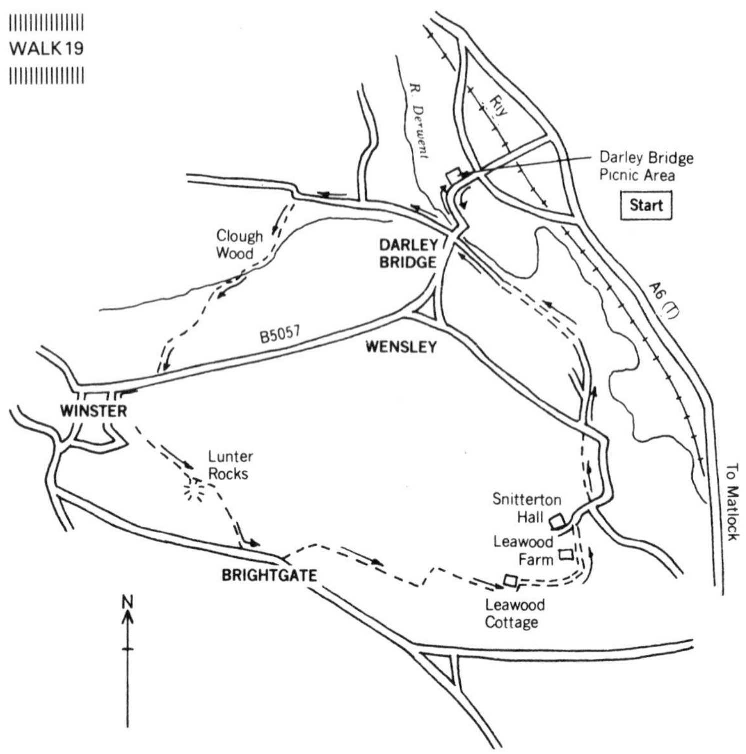

set in the road and is used as an information centre.

Turn left at the Market House and left at the Bowling Green Inn to pass through a stile into a field beyond the toilets. Turn right to follow a wall, then cross to the far corner of the field and pass through a gap in the wall. Bear right up the hill to the wall stile set amongst trees, then follow the path bearing left beyond the stile in the wall corner and walk to Lunter Rocks, now visible on the near horizon.

Take the stile below the rocks and walk along the wood bottom. Pass through a gateway beyond the wood and continue in the same direction with the wall to your left. In the fourth field bear right and cross to the far corner. Cross four fields in this direction and then bear left and follow the wall for two fields. Cross to the far corner to join a road. In most cases throughout the walk there are stiles and from Winster the direction is generally in a series of slight zigzags. This too is a mining area and there are hundreds of filled-in shafts.

Turn left and walk along the road to the hamlet of Brightgate. After passing through the hamlet and at a pronounced right bend in the road, turn left into a field at a stile. Turn right and follow the wall over four fields. This is part of the boundary of the Peak District National Park. In the fifth field turn left and cross the field and in the corner turn right onto a cart track to descend to Leawood Cottage, continuing down to Leawood Farm and on to Snitterton Hall, identifiable from above.

Turn right and at the narrow road junction with a motor road turn left at the sign 'Public Footpath to Wensley and Winster' to cross the fields and avoid the road, which is soon rejoined. Turn left, then right along Ashton Lane. Take the second turn right at Apple Tree Cottage and eventually follow the narrow, metalled road across the fields back into Darley Bridge.

LOOKS GOOD WALK NEAR CROMFORD GRADIENTS

MAP 24

BLACK ROCK

WALK 20

★

4 miles (6.5 km)

OS sheet 119, White Peak

Wirksworth is an old lead mining town completely overshadowed by the massive quarry above it. The town is not entered on the walk, but from the high point of the walk the town is seen as from a bird's-eye view, in almost its entirety. Along the northern side is the High Peak Trail, the converted railway track which eventually descends east, terminating at the Cromford Canal. The walk starts at the Black Rock picnic area (SK 291 557), where there are several scenic car parks. This is almost at the summit of the B5036 rising from Cromford to Wirksworth.

Walk east along the High Peak Trail. Black Rock is high to the right. Soon there are bird's-eye views over Cromford. A solitary, grand house can be seen to the east of the town. This is Willersley Castle, once the home of Sir Richard Arkwright. Along the trail an old engine shed is reached. This once housed the machinery for making the 1 in 8 ascent and descent possible. On the descent of the trail turn right at the sign 'Public Footpath Intake Lane Cromford Alderwasley', taking a path that soon joins a track, which has passed under the trail.

Turn right along the track and when a field's length away from a farm, turn right through a stile and follow a wall edge to join a grassed track. Turn right up the track, which at times becomes a path, and walk in almost a straight line, passing a farm to join a motor road overlooking Wirksworth. Turn right and just before reaching houses turn right through a stile at a

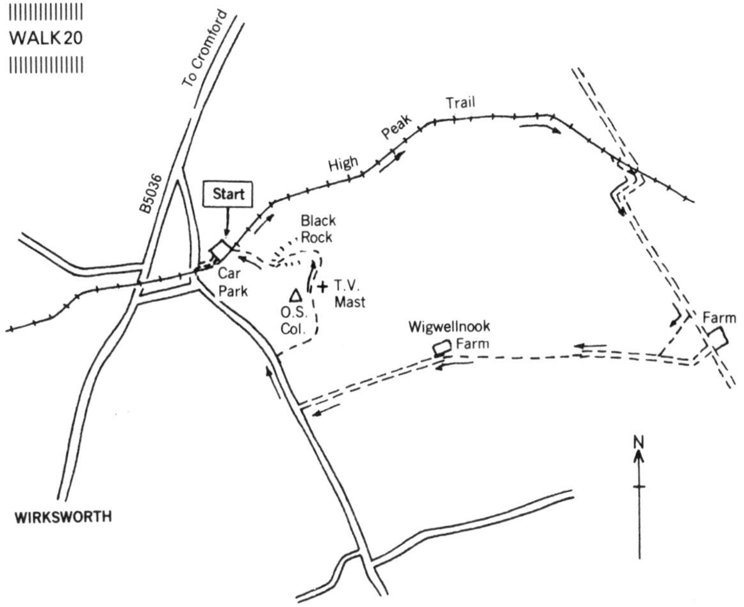

public footpath sign. Climb the hill directly to a wood corner near a television mast that has been visible for some time.

Take the path through the trees to the mast and an ordnance column, from where the best views of Wirksworth can be had. Continue on the path that descends to Black Rock, seen at the beginning of the walk, and which leads to the High Peak Trail picnic area.

MATLOCK
DON'T KNOW

HEIGHTS OF ABRAHAM

WALK 21

★

4 miles (6.5 km)

OS sheet 119, White Peak

Matlock and Matlock Bath, like Buxton, are now not visited for their health-giving mineral waters, but still attract visitors in their thousands. There are many attractions for the tourist, with Matlock Bath apparently providing the majority of sight-seeing places. The only level ground is perhaps between Matlock and Matlock Bath by the side of the A6 which closely follows the river Derwent. Consequently most walks are climbs, although not of too severe a nature.

The walk is primarily from Matlock to the Heights of Abraham, which has its connection with Wolfe's dramatic victory at Quebec and his unfortunate death in 1759. This is a commanding viewpoint above Matlock Bath and can be reached from there, but not in as gentle a gradient. The walk starts at Matlock Bridge (SK 298 602), built in the 15th century, but widened in the present century.

Walk away from the town, turning right up Snitterton Road at the Royal Bank of Scotland. One hundred and fifty yards up the road turn left at the sign 'Public Footpath to Masson and Bonsall', up a metalled track leading to a field and up the field hollow. When a narrow lane is reached turn left at the sign 'Public Footpath Matlock Bath 1¼'. This is a good place to see Matlock spread out below. On the skyline on the opposite side of the valley is the sprawling mass of Riber Castle, now the home of Riber Zoo but built by John Smedley, one of Matlock's prominent mid-Victorian personalities. He was a textile magnate who introduced new machinery to the area in the middle of the 19th century and who built Smedley's Hydro, a large building seen across the town. The Hydro is now used by the county council.

When the lane turns right to a farm, continue forward instead at the sign 'Public Footpath Matlock Bath 1', following the contour of the hillside. This joins an old road at a chapel. This is the church of St John the Baptist, a High Church chapel of ease to the parish church designed by Sir Guy Dowber in 1897 and endowed by Mrs Harris of The Rocks nearby.

Turn right up the hill and just before the road enters a private house, turn right at the sign 'Public Footpath Heights of Abraham' to follow the wall side, turning left at the wall

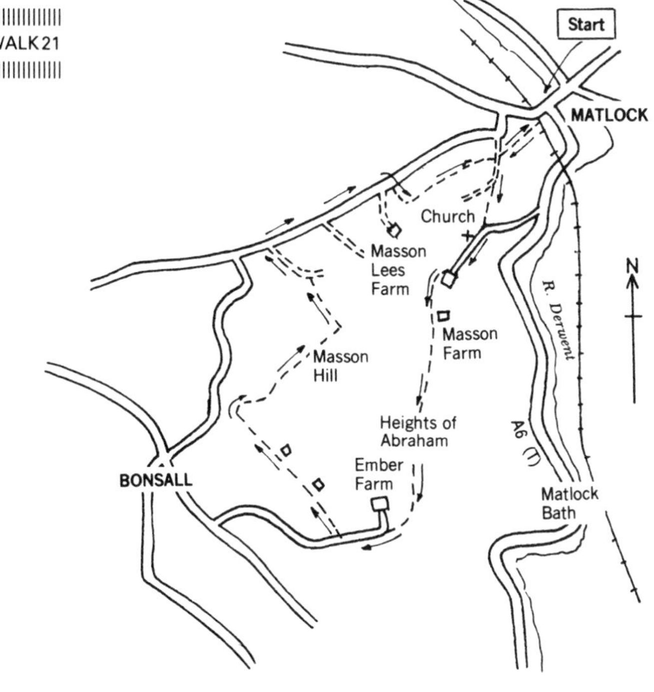

corner at another sign 'Public Footpath No 77 to Ember Farm and Bonsall'. Take the field path to climb to the right of a farm and later up the hill at a footpath sign. Ahead can be seen Prospect Tower and although the path appears to go well to the right of the tower, it eventually veers left to arrive at the entrance to the Heights of Abraham and the tower.

Prospect Tower is a Victorian stone-built construction with a somewhat frightening, interior, spiral, open stone staircase leading to a small tower top from which are admirable views over Matlock Dale.

From the Heights entrance continue on the path up the wood and when the track splits take the left fork. This is a well used path eventually reaching a track at another sign 'Public Footpath to Bonsall'. Follow the sign to join a farm road and shortly after a private track on the right, just before a small building on the left, turn right over a stile across fields to two standing stones. From here pass to the left of two lots of farm buildings. After a second set the way is to the far left corner, around the corner of which a concrete path is joined to pass a ruin and on to another concrete path.

Turn right up the hill on the path and when the concrete ceases turn left up the hill. After two stiles the path veers left aiming to the left of a limestone wall. Follow the wall beyond its corner to enter a narrow field. In front is Masson Hill, the highest point in the area, from which are even better views than from the Heights of Abraham. Follow the path to the left of the hill to the field overlooking the valley. This is a reclaimed area from limestone workings.

Turn left and walk to the left of the workings to join a quarry road and on to the motor road ahead. Turn right and walk as far as the drive to Masson Lees Farm. One field below the drive climb a narrow stile to enter a field. At the end of the field to the left pass through a stile and walk down the left side of a wall for several fields. The path eventually reaches the Matlock Bath path, with a short descent into Matlock.

THE DERBYSHIRE COUNTRYSIDE

Although a great deal of the Derbyshire countryside goes under the plough, it is not all farmland and the idea of field after field filled with growing crops is false. Some areas are owned by the Forestry Commission; elsewhere is land and water controlled by a particular water authority; while the lead mining industry, long departed, has left its relics and traces and mineral workings are very evident in parts of the county.

These last nine walks explore several of the different aspects of the Derbyshire countryside.

WALK 22

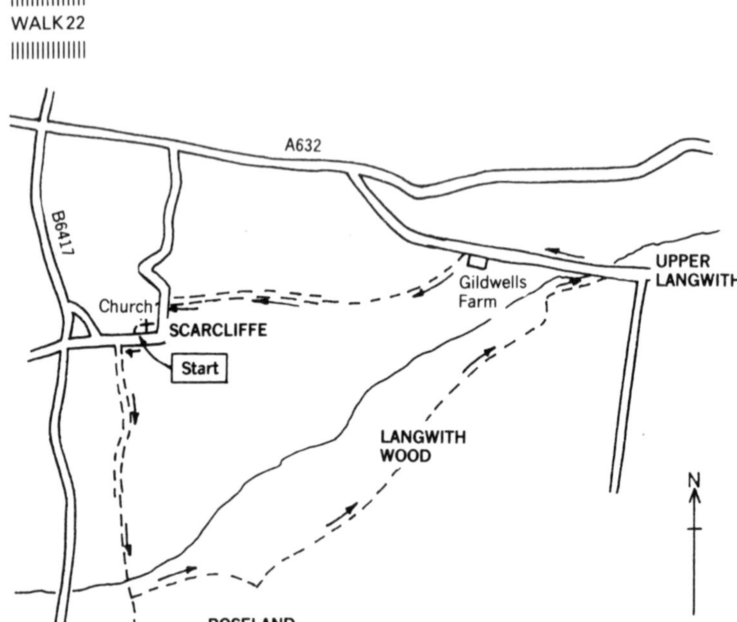
A632
B6417
Church
SCARCLIFFE
Start
Gildwells Farm
UPPER LANGWITH
LANGWITH WOOD
ROSELAND WOOD
N

TOO FAR AWAY

LANGWITH WOOD

WALK 22

★

4 miles (6.5 km)

OS sheet 120, SK 46/56

In Scarcliffe church is the alabaster tomb of Lady Constantine de Frecheville, who lived in the 12th century. It is said that she, with her daughter, still wanders through the woods near Scarcliffe. Scarcliffe itself, although so near a mining area, is more a rural village, having a church with Norman connections. The extensive woods to the south are largely closed to walkers, but there are a few through paths open to the public. The walk is through part of Roseland Wood and the length of Langwith Wood. The walk starts at Scarcliffe church (SK 496 688).

Walk west through the village and take the first left turn after the telephone kiosk along a track. When the track divides take the left fork along the edge of a field to cross a stream to enter Roseland Wood. When the path forks near a gate and fields, turn left and follow a well-trodden path through the wood, then along a field edge. When a track is joined turn left into Langwith Wood.

When several paths join, continue forward, bearing slightly right, to walk through the length of the wood, emerging near fields to join a road at Upper Langwith. Turn left along the road to descend to the bottom of the hill, then ascend the hill ahead. Just past a farm turn left into a field at a public footpath sign and climb the short hill to a fence visible from below. Climb the stile in the fence corner and walk on the left side of a fence. After ¼ mile the path joins a track and continues towards Scarcliffe. When a road is reached cross the playing fields to the church.

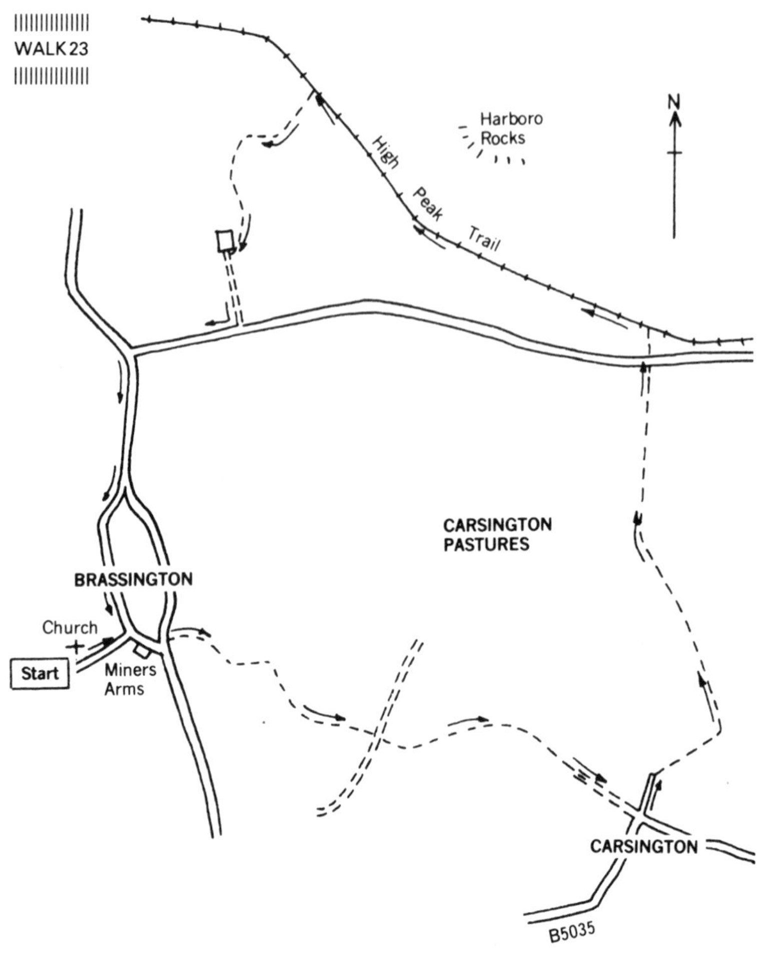
WALK 23
Harboro
Rocks
N
High
Peak
Trail
CARSINGTON
PASTURES
BRASSINGTON
Church
Start
Miners
Arms
CARSINGTON
B5035

CARSINGTON PASTURES

WALK 23

★

5 miles (8 km)

OS sheet 119, White Peak

Between Brassington and Carsington is an area of land that is different to any other part of the district. For some unknown reason the land missed the Enclosure Acts and consequently there are no limestone walls crisscrossing the undulating ground. The bumps and hollows are all man made, for this was a mining area, mainly for lead, although sand, clay, barytes, dolomite, limestone and probably other minerals were sought after. There are still quarries and works here and there, though the main industry today is agriculture.

Brassington was a mining village, an abiding testimony being The Miners Arms, one of the village inns. The walk starts from Brassington church (SK 230 543), a building tracing its history to the Norman era. It has a Norman tower and porch. Other parts are Norman with a mixture of Victorian architecture.

Walk past The Miners Arms to the T-junction and pass into a field at the sign 'Public Footpath Carsington 1½'. Cross the centre of two fields diagonally and up the wall side of the third field and through a stile. Turn right and walk along the wall side at first, then climb the hill leaving the wall, to follow the path around overgrown mine workings. This was Nickalum mine. After reaching the brow of the hill descend the other side to join a track to the right of a small building. Cross the track and enter the field at the sign 'Public Footpath to Carsington'. Cross the field and climb the hill ahead to the left of a copse near the field corner. Cross the next field corner to join a grass track from old workings and descend by it into Carsington, at first veering left to miss the fields below. Carsington is a smaller village with an embattled church rebuilt in 1648.

At the crossroads turn left at the sign 'Public Footpath to Ible and Grangemill', passing between houses and through the garden of the top house to enter the hillside by way of a low gate. Climb the steep hill bearing right towards the thick wood, and on reaching the fence follow it. When the fence reaches a wall do not climb the stile, but bear left with the wall and follow it as far as the motor road. This is the eastern boundary of Carsington Pastures.

Cross the road and a short field and turn left onto the High Peak Trail. This is the track of the former Cromford and High Peak Railway, disused for some time, but reclaimed for use by walkers, cyclists and pony trekkers. Along this section are items of industrial interest: a brickworks, old slurry ponds, old workings with ruined buildings and to the right Harboro Rocks, with caves where it is reputed miners with their families lived.

Just before a narrow, wooded cutting turn left over a stile at the sign 'Public Footpath Brassington'. Cross two fields with a wall to your left. Pass through a stile, turn right along the wall side on a grass track, veering left and eventually passing through a small farm onto a farm road. At the motor road ahead turn right, then left at a T-junction and finally take the first right turn to Brassington.

PROB. TOO FAR ?

MAP 24

RAINSTER ROCKS

WALK 24

6½ miles (10.5 km)

OS sheet 119, White Peak

To the west of Brassington is a prominently high outcrop of rocks popular with climbers and families, although it is unnecessary to take a rope to climb to the top. There is an easier route round the back. The walk starts from Brassington church (SK 230 543).

Walk south-west away from the village centre and at Ye Olde Gate Inn turn right up a snicket. When the narrow walled track splits, turn right joining a narrow road. Turn right and very shortly left into a field at the sign 'Public Footpath Longcliffe', obliquely ascending the hill on a path. Over the brow of the hill Rainster Rocks can be seen in the middle distance. Enter a walled track and turn left. After one field turn right through a stile and walk directly towards the rocks, at first passing under an outcrop of rock.

From the rocks walk to the road visible from the rocks, turn right and walk down the road as far as a T-junction. Cross the road and after passing through a stile climb the hill on a grass track. After passing over the brow of the hill, bear slightly left off the track to the distant wall corner, passing a small standing stone on the way. Beyond the wall corner stile, descend the hill to a small isolated church in between a track and motor road. This is a restored Norman church. Nearby is the hamlet of Ballidon. Turn left along the track and when it turns sharp right to a barn continue forward to a motor road. Turn right and after 30 yards turn left through a stile into a field.

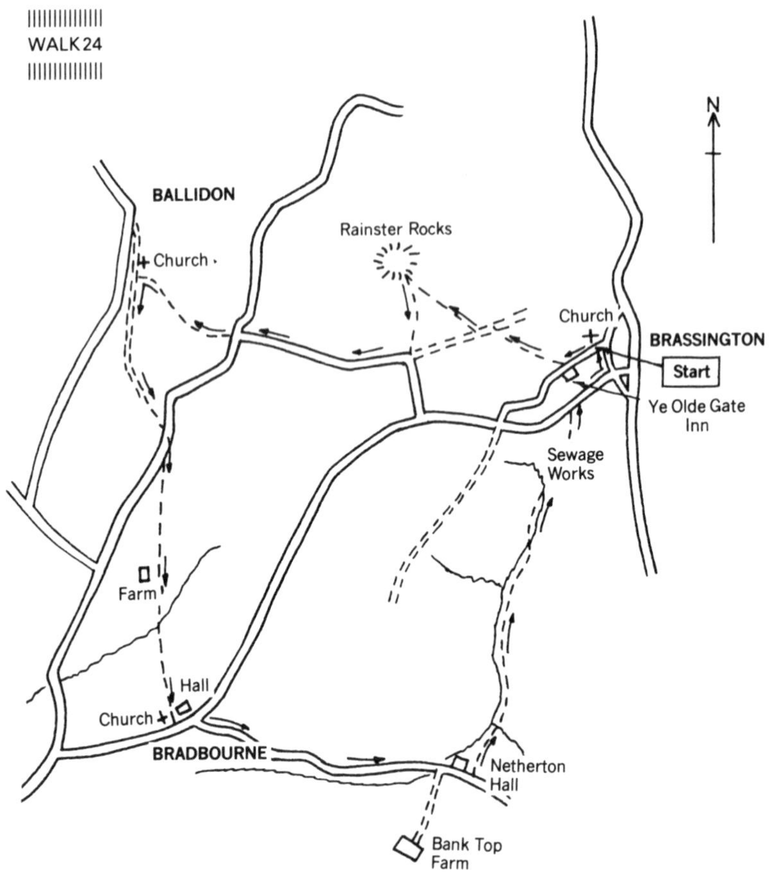

In the distance can be seen the square tower of Bradbourne church. Walk directly towards it. After the first two fields keep to the right of a hedge, then across the middle of the fields ahead, but to the left of farm buildings, finally climbing the hill to the church to the right of a copse and hedge to pass through the church grounds onto a motor road.

Bradbourne church has Saxon and Norman interests and near the gate is an old cross. The Buckston family are well commemorated, including Thomas Buckston who died in 1811. He had been one of the oldest officers in the forces and had fought at Culloden. The hall next door is Elizabethan.

Pass the hall and turn right at the post office on the Carsington road until reaching Netherton Hall, the large house on the left side up a incline and beyond Bank Top Farm. Fifty yards past the hall turn left into a field at the sign 'Public Footpath Carsington'. Take the direction of this sign rather than towards Brassington seen in the distance. After another narrow stream is crossed the Carsington path departs right, but the Brassington path continues over fields and stiles, never far from the stream to the left. Further upstream the path crosses the stream and continues up the other side until a sewage farm is reached. Pass round two sides and at the end of the fence turn right through a stile and walk diagonally across the field to the far corner. Walk up the field side and re-enter Brassington village. Turn right and return to the church.

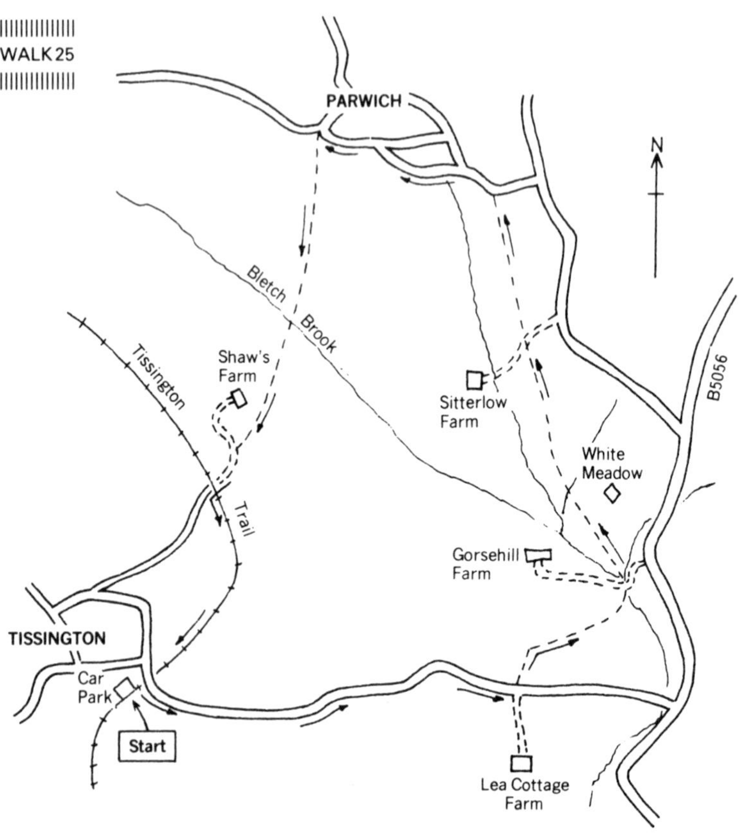
WALK 25
PARWICH
N
Bletch Brook
Tissington
Trail
Shaw's Farm
Sitterlow Farm
B5056
White Meadow
Gorsehill Farm
TISSINGTON
Car Park
Start
Lea Cottage Farm

LOOKS NICE GRADIENTS

MAP 24

TISSINGTON AND PARWICH

WALK 25

★

5 miles (8 km)

OS sheet 119, White Peak

Parwich is a village built near old earthworks where many finds have been made. Tissington is better known, being the home of the Fitzherberts and having several impressive houses. It is also the village with the oldest of the well dressings and on Ascension Day each year thousands visit the village to see the five wells dressed to commemorate the time 600 years ago when the waters never failed. The walk starts at the Tissington Trail car park (SK 178 521), once the station for the village.

Walk to the road and turn right. Shortly after a gate crosses the road, turn left across a field at the sign 'Public Footpath to Parwich'. In the field corner take the right of two gates and descend the hill to the left of a wall to join a farm road visible from the top. Turn right on it and after crossing a cattle grid turn left through a stile to cross fields in the shallow valley bottom, bearing gradually right to take the right-hand valley. Along the way a narrow stream is crossed and shortly afterwards a farm road. After this continue walking across the middle of the fields towards Parwich seen ahead. On reaching a motor road walk into Parwich.

After passing the church turn left on the Alsop-en-le-Dale road and at a right-hand bend near a cave pass into a field, at the sign 'Public Footpath to Tissington 2', to climb the hill to a stile seen ahead. Climb on to the middle of the next hedge above, then walk on the left side of a hedge, taking the stile on the left side of another hedge.

The way ahead can now be seen. The path descends to a bridge over Bletch Brook and climbs directly up the hill beyond, passing well to the left of a farm halfway up the hill. When the path joins a farm road turn left and walk on it to an old railway bridge crossing the Tissington Trail. Join the trail and walk back to the car park.

GOOD WALK MAP 24

GRADIENTS

FENNY BENTLEY

WALK 26

★

4 miles (6.5 km)

OS sheet 119, White Peak, SK 04/14

Fenny Bentley is the first village north of Ashbourne on the A515, an attractive place with a much restored church enclosing monuments and mementoes of the Beresford family. Thomas Beresford was the first one at Fenny Bentley and had fought at Agincourt. The walk starts at Tissington Trail car park (SK 178 521), the converted station on the eastern side of Tissington.

Walk south on the Tissington Trail, passing through the Thorpe picnic site. From this point the old track makes a long left bend. At the place where the direction of the bend changes from left to right, locate a signpost to Fenny Bentley and leave the track, descending to a bridge over a stream directly below the track. At the other side of the stream climb the hill with a hedge to your right. After negotiating a stile at the top cross the next field heading for the right of a farm just ahead. Beyond the stile below the farm aim next for a small barn and beyond this for the right of terraced houses. The path now passes between the houses and a school to the church. Walk round the church to the A515.

To the right of the telephone kiosk near an old school is the signpost 'Public Footpath Tissington 2'. Walk along the track and cross the nearby stream to ascend to a field. Over to the right is Fenny Bentley Old Hall, a 17th century manor house with a medieval tower. This was the home of one of the Beresfords and a regular visitor was Izaak Walton.

WALK 26

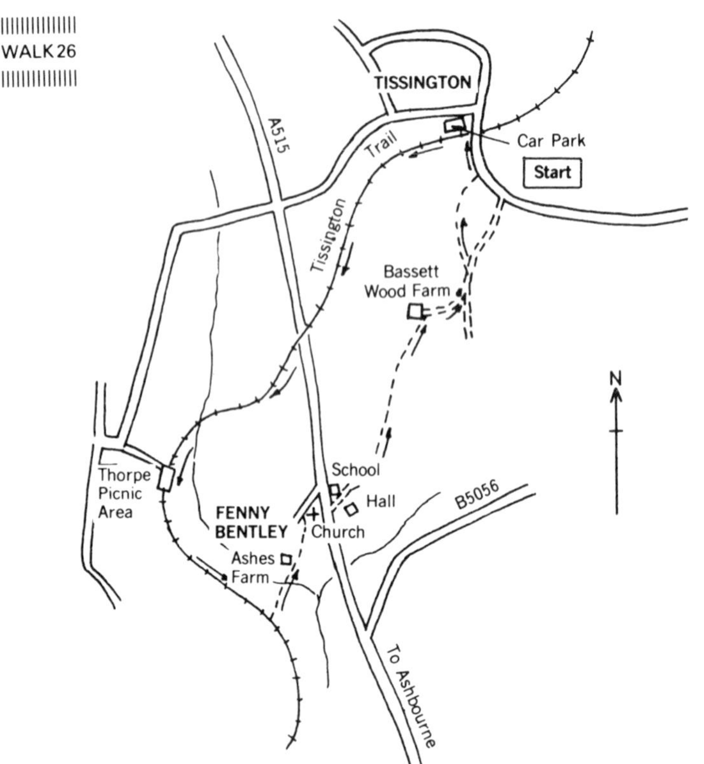

Enter the field, keeping to the right of a hedge, and just past a house turn left up the field to climb steadily for a few fields, keeping fairly close to a hedge on your left until Bassett Wood Farm is reached. Turn right along the farm road and after passing another farm road joining from the right, and at a point where two prominent trees stand sentinel one at each side of the road, turn left over a fence and walk alongside a hedge on your left. Beyond the next field corner cross the field diagonally to join a narrow motor road. Turn left along the road, soon to arrive at the Tissington Trail entrance.

BIG WALL GRADIENTS COULD BE GOOD MAP 2 59

KIRK IRETON, BIGGIN AND IDRIDGEHAY

WALK 27

★

5½ miles (9 km)

OS sheet 119, White Peak, SK 24/34

This is a walk over fields, along quiet country lanes and through peaceful villages around The Mountain, a peak which hardly justifies its given name as it is but 795 ft above sea level. The walk is from the charming village of Kirk Ireton a few miles south of Wirksworth. There are several interesting historical buildings, including Barley Mow, a 17th century twin-gabled house, a fascinating church with Norman remains and an 18th century brick farm house. The walk starts at the church (SK 269 502).

Walk through the village and at the T-junction turn left on the Blackwall road. At the road fork ahead, turn right and take the first left turn along Field Lane. The track ends at a farm and the walk continues past the left side of the farm and to the right of the hedge directly beyond a single-storeyed building to the left of the farm. Take the stile in the bottom left corner of the field, continuing down the hill beyond and over the stream by a bridge directly beneath an isolated house. Climb the hill ahead to the left of the facing hedge which soon turns a corner. After climbing a stile at the field's end, bear left to a gap in the opposing hedge and head for the right-hand end of the poultry factory seen to the left. Pass to the other side of the farm to join a road crossing a stream. At a T-junction turn right and after that keep taking left turns at road junctions, passing the small villages of Biggin and Millington Green.

WALK 27

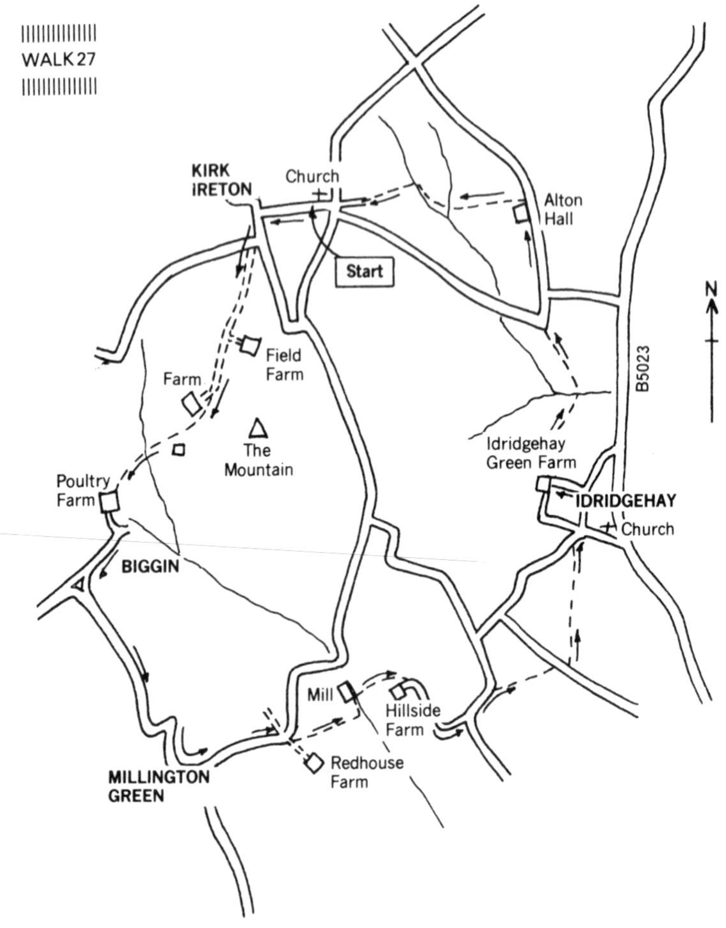

KIRK IRETON
Church
Start
Alton Hall
Field Farm
Farm
The Mountain
Poultry Farm
BIGGIN
Idridgehay Green Farm
IDRIDGEHAY
Church
B5023
N
Mill
Hillside Farm
Redhouse Farm
MILLINGTON GREEN

After passing Lanehead Farm look for tracks at either side of the road. The left is guarded by a gate, the one on the right goes to a farm. Take the track on the right, but leave it immediately, heading for the opposite corner of the field. In the field beyond keep in the same direction towards a single wire carrying pole, descending to a stream. To the left is an old mill. Climb the fence by the stream and walk towards the old building, crossing the stream by a bridge just before the mill. Climb the hill at the other side of the stream in the direction indicated by a public bridleway sign, entering a tree-lined overgrown path at the top of which is a stile and beyond this a house. Walk to the far corner of the field to join a track descending to the house. Take the track until a motor road is reached.

Turn left on the road and after passing under low power lines turn right into a field at the stile next to the second gate on the right. Climb the field to the stile in the opposite corner and again cross to the opposite corner to join a road. Turn right for one field length and turn left through the first gate into a field. Walk to the right of a hedge for two fields, climbing a stile at the end of the second field. Follow the hedge on the left, taking the stile just to the right of the field corner, and keep to the left side of the next hedge. At its end cross to the right-hand corner of the next field to join a road. Idridgehay church is just to the right. Turn right and walk into Idridgehay, which is another attractive village with a mid 19th century church and one or two old houses.

Cross the crossroads and turn left at the next fork, walking to a farm at the end of the narrow road. Pass through the small farmyard and turn right in the field beyond, walking by the side of a hedge on the right for two fields. Cross a bridge and a stile near the bridge and turn left up a field to a gate to enter a road. Turn right and then first left to walk to Alton Hall up the road. Alton Hall with several other buildings is by the roadside. Well over to the right and not seen from the road are the parklands of Alton Manor. The manor house overlooks a lake and the park.

Just past Alton Hall turn left at the sign 'Public Footpath Kirk Ireton' into a field. Over to the right in the distance can be seen the buildings of Kirk Ireton. If this direction is maintained over the fields ahead, a stile will be found in the wood at the bottom of the third field. Cross a bridge over the stream at the other side of the stile and climb the hill ahead to cross another stream at the end of the wood on the left. Bear left directly up the hill and to the right of a hedge to a stile near an overgrown old ruin, passing on to Kirk Ireton.

TOO FAR OUT

SOMERSAL HERBERT

WALK 28

★

4 miles (6.5 km)

OS sheet 128, SK 03/13

Somersal Hall has long associations with the Fitzherbert family who occupied it continuously from the 13th century. It is a half-timbered building with ornamental gables standing in its own grounds close to the road and therefore easily seen from the gates. Next door is the church, largely rebuilt a century ago, but having a Norman font and an ancient cross. The walk starts from Marston Montgomery (SK 135 379), another charming village with ancient lineage. Manor Farm is half timbered and the church has a history going back to the Normans. The walk to Somersal Herbert is a gentle rural arc across fields and streams.

Take the Doveridge road. Fifty yards down the road climb over a stile on the left and walk the boundary of the house. At the corner of the property turn right and cross the field to climb over a stile. Walk along the left side of a hedge in the field beyond, gradually leaving it to cross a bridge in the opposing hedge. Climb the next field with a fence on the right and at the field end climb the fence ahead and walk up the field, heading for the right of a farm at the top of the hill.

Descend the field to the right of the farm buildings and the hedge below. After crossing a bridge at the bottom, bear slightly right to walk along the right-hand side of the hedge, crossing three fields in the process. When it is no longer possible to follow the way ahead to a farm, turn right across the field to join a farm track. Turn left and pass the farm, continuing on the

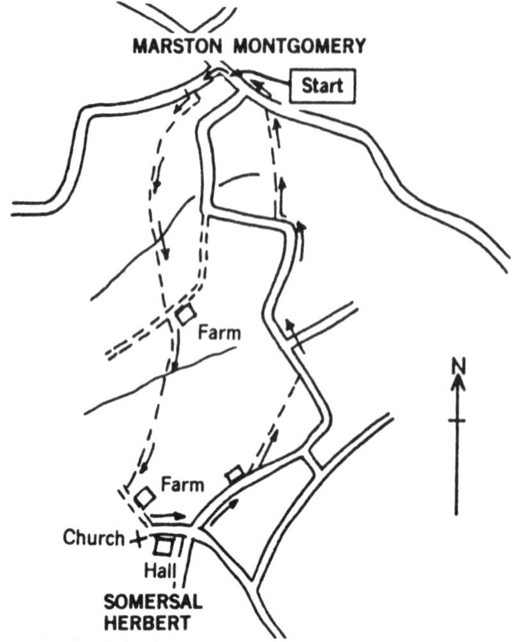

road beyond into Somersal Herbert. The village consists of the hall, church, farms and little else.

At the crossroads turn left and just past the first farm turn left into a field. The house visible across the fields should be the aim, emerging on to a road to its right. Turn left and walk along the road for just over ½ mile. After a sharp left bend pass through the gate immediately after the third telegraph pole. Follow the hedge on the right and after another gate, cross the middle of the next two fields. Cross the next field to a roadside gate and turn left along the road into Marston Montgomery.

TOO FAR OUT

ROBIN WOOD

WALK 29

★

4½ miles (7 km)

OS sheet 128, SK 22/32

Robin Wood is owned by the Forestry Commission and is mainly a dense plantation with one bridleway through its middle and a footpath inside part of one side. It lies not far from the picturesque town of Melbourne, but the walk starts at the pretty village of Ticknall, 3 miles south-west of Melbourne. The starting place is the Methodist chapel (SK 353 241), which is in a cul-de-sac just off the Ingleby road.

Walk to the end of the cul-de-sac and through the two wooden posts barring further vehicular progress. Turn left and pass a narrow gate into a field. Follow a track bearing right, soon to reduce to a path, and follow it as it goes along the right-hand side of a hedge. At the field corner climb over a fence and continue on the path, which is now more pronounced. The path passes a public footpath sign implanted in a hedge, then follows low power lines well to the left of farm buildings. When the power lines split at a wall corner follow the left lines to enter a wood near a wall corner. After the short walk through the plantation, and after passing through a gate into a field, bear slightly left and walk at the right foot of a small hill and afterwards to the left of a walled copse enclosing a small lake. At the field end near farm buildings turn left on a track, and after passing through a gate turn right over a fence to pass to the right of a small lake and on to a track.

Turn right on the track following the edge of a plantation, eventually joining a road near a power pylon. Walk along the

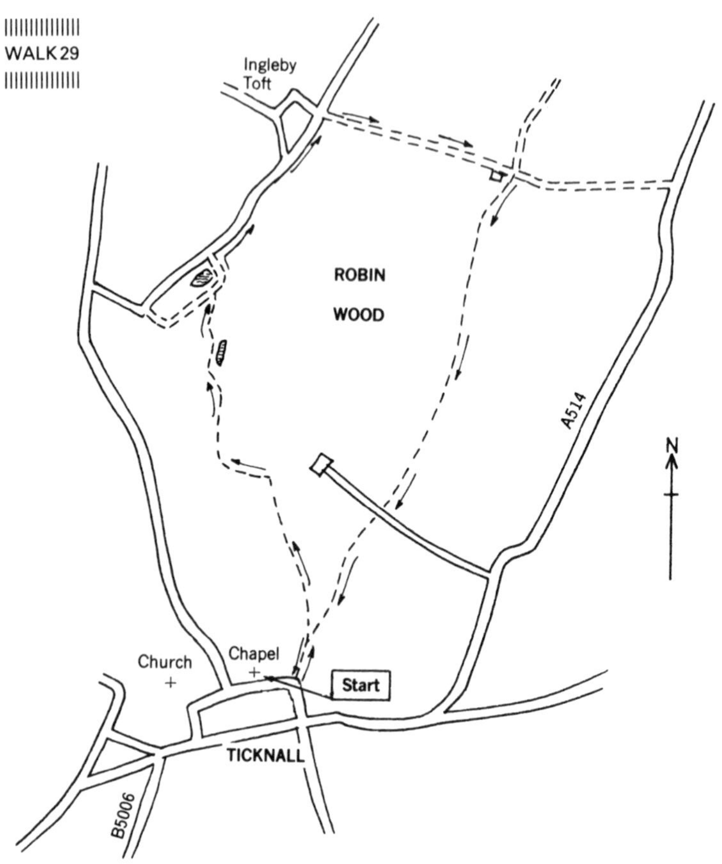
WALK 29
Ingleby
Toft
ROBIN
WOOD
A514
N
Church
Chapel
Start
TICKNALL
B5006

road and turn right at a public bridleway sign. In the distance can be seen the twisting ribbon of the river Trent. Follow the track as it climbs a hill at the edge of Robin Wood.

At a house just beyond the wood turn right into a field at the sign 'Public Footpath Ticknall 2' and walk along the plantation edge. In the fourth field climb the fence stile at a post marked 'footpath' and continue to follow the plantation, this time inside the fence. At the wood end climb the fence stile and cross the middle of the field to join a lane near a water trough. Enter the field opposite by the gate to the right and walk towards Ticknall, seen in the distance to the right of a hedge, eventually rejoining the first path taken. This will involve climbing a fence before the last field.

MUCH TOO FAR OUT.

COTON IN THE ELMS

WALK 30

★

6 miles (9.5 km)

OS sheet 128, SK 21/31

Several villages in the southernmost part of the county are visited on this walk, through an area which is largely agricultural, but pleasantly wooded. The first village is Coton in the Elms, having an early Victorian church with a handsomely slender spire, and the walk starts here (SK 243 155).

Walk south and turn left on Elms Road at the Shoulder of Mutton and left on Burton Road at the T-junction. After passing the drive to Longfurlong Farm take the first farm track on the left, passing a farm and continuing across the field beyond. When the corner of the field on the left is reached, climb over a stile and continue across the next field towards houses. At the next field corner climb the stile on the right and cross the field to the far left corner, passing on to a track and beyond that the road. This is Rosliston. Rosliston is about the same size as Coton, but the church is older, parts dating to the 14th century, but mainly rebuilt in 1819.

Turn left on the road and after a short walk turn right onto a track at the sign 'Public Footpath to Caldwell', passing a children's playground. At a sharp left bend continue instead in the original direction on a path across a field, passing a wood to enter the small village of Caldwell at a small church. Caldwell is the village; Cauldwell is the parish.

Caldwell has Saxon origins, a small Norman church and Caldwell Hall. The hall is early 18th century, an impressive building once having a moat and several owners, but now a

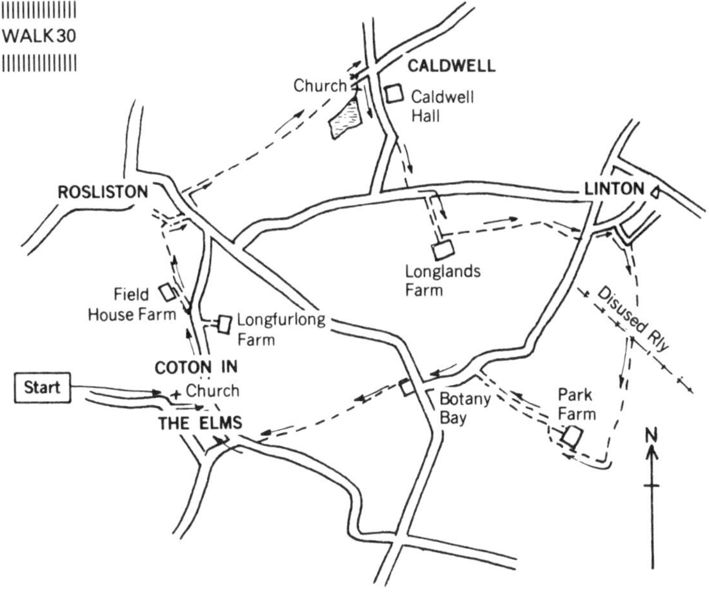

specialist school.

Turn right at the crossroads, passing Caldwell Hall, and at the first sharp right bend pass into a field, crossing to the opposite corner towards distant buildings. Join the road beyond the field, turn left and after 100 yards turn right on the drive leading to Longlands Farm seen from the road. Just before the farm buildings turn left into a field and bypass the farm. Pass to the right of a wood and across the middle of the field ahead. In the next field bear right to the far opposite corner to join a road. Turn left and walk towards Linton ahead.

Take the first right turn and the next first right turn into an estate. When the road turns sharp left, bear right to enter a field at the sign 'Public Footpath Grangewood 1½'. Walk alongside the hedge on the right and beyond a low elevated pipe pass under a railway bridge. Bear left to walk on the left side of a hedge. After 60 yards climb a stile to walk with the hedge on your left for two fields. At the end of the second field turn right to a farm, passing round the left side to join the farm road and walk to a motor road.

Turn left and walk into Botany Bay, which probably has connections with the more notorious penal colony. Botany Bay consists of a handful of houses. From here Coton church spire can be seen as a guide in the distance.

At the T-junction turn right on the road, but enter the first field and walk around the perimeter of a garden to strike directly away from the house dated 1875, at the field's edges. At the end of the second field on the left pass round the right-hand side of a small copse. At the field end cross a short corner of the field ahead, turning right to enter another field and walk across to the opposite corner in a direction aimed halfway between the church and houses to its left. A road is joined at the houses and the village of Coton in the Elms is soon reached.